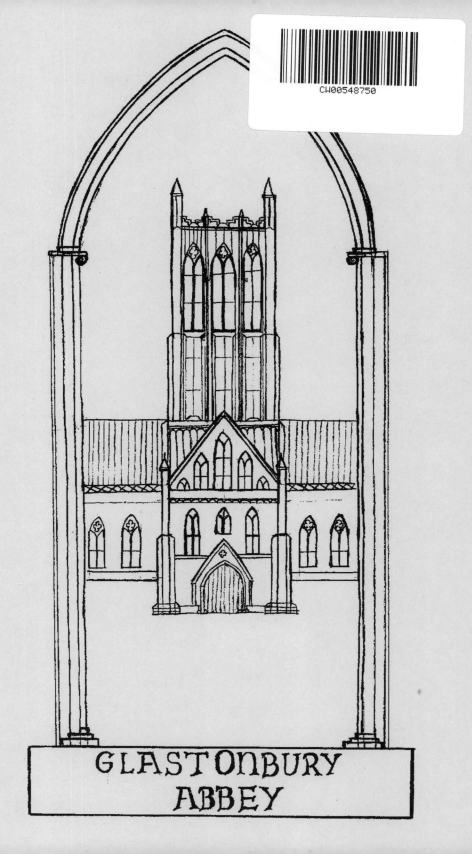

GLASTONBURY
ABBEY

Charles

With my good wishes,

Peter

The Wealth and Estates

of Glastonbury Abbey

at the Dissolution

in

1539

Peter Clery

2003

First published in 2003 by
Curlew Publishers, Curlew Court
Guy's Head, Sutton Bridge
Lincolnshire
PE12 9QQ
Email curlew@pclery.freeserve.co.uk

ISBN 0-9545101-0-0

Printed in Great Britain by Antony Rowe Ltd, Chippenham,
Wiltshire SN14 6LH

ACKNOWLEDGEMENTS and AUTHOR'S NOTE

I wish particularly to thank Dr Michael Thompson of Leicester University for his time, care and aid with translations and the unstinting way he has helped this book. Also major thanks to my cousin Margaret McGregor for her painstaking work on the PRO material. Thanks also to Ruth Taylor-Briggs of Birmingham University who diligently shouldered a large part of the Beere transcribing.

My late Uncle Edwin George kindly found the BRO note on gold hoarding.

David Bromwich, Somerset County librarian, introduced me to the Beere texts - my thanks to him for original ideas and factual information. Thanks also to Michael McGarvie for his encouragement and help in organising access to certain Beere texts and to the London Society of Antiquaries for similar help and arranging permission to use texts. The staff of the British Library, Public Records Office and Cambridge University Library have been very helpful, as have been Rural Partners Ltd who produced the location plan of the estates. The Public Records Office has also given permission for the reproduction of texts which is gratefully acknowledged.

Barbara Harvey read a draft and made helpful suggestions, as did Penny Stokes who also very kindly provided colour photographs. My thanks to all of them. Also to Robin Clery for his impressions of the Abbey in its prime and to the Abbey Trustees and Matthew Clements for permission to sketch from Nigel Gaffney's model of the abbey and to use other Abbey material.

Finally, my special thanks to Elizabeth H.S who has patiently and skilfully kept the word processor and spreadsheets in order and the project on track to completion and to my sister Elizabeth C for her proof reading of the script.

Thanks to all but the responsibility for the work and errors therein lie entirely with me.

Readers may well have better knowledge than I on some of the subject matter of this book. I would be most grateful for any additional material which could be incorporated in a future edition.

Finally, any reader who would like further information on any of the occupiers listed in Appendix D are invited to contact the publishers.

Peter Clery

THE WEALTH and ESTATES of GLASTONBURY ABBEY
at the DISSOLUTION in 1539

CONTENTS

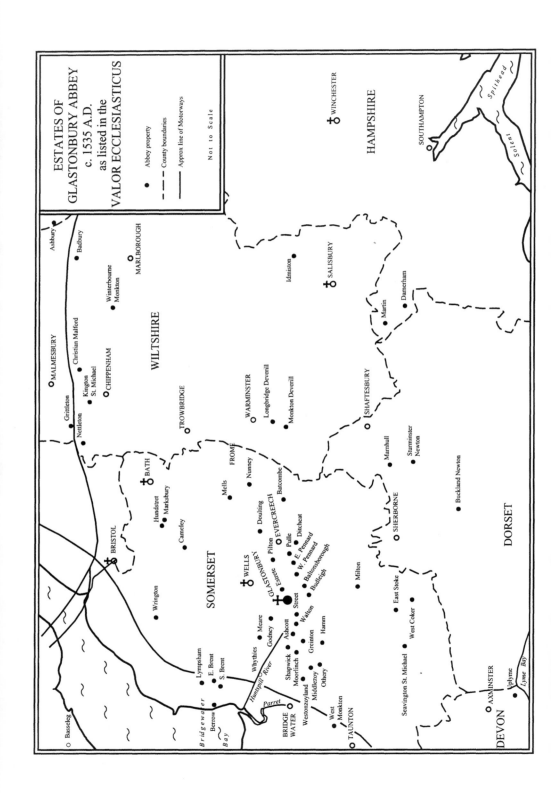

ESTATES OF
GLASTONBURY ABBEY
c. 1535 A.D.
as listed in the
VALOR ECCLESIASTICUS

• Abbey property
‒ ‒ ‒ County boundaries
——— Approx line of Motorways

Not to Scale

The WEALTH and ESTATES of GLASTONBURY ABBEY at the DISSOLUTION in 1539

Introduction

The acquisition of monastic land by Henry VIII in the years leading up to 1540 was the biggest peacetime land transaction in English history. The Benedictine abbeys of Glastonbury and Westminster[1] were the two wealthiest monastic houses, each enjoying **an annual income close to £4000 gross (equivalent to atleast some £1.2 million in today's money).** However, Glastonbury owned the most land, all of which passed (along with the treasure and sale proceeds of furniture and other goods) *'into the Kynge's hands'* in 1539. The abbey owned much treasure but most of the wealth lay in land and these broad acres are the main subject of this book.

Glastonbury assets, though vast, probably represented only about 3% of the total monastic wealth taken by Henry Vlll.

Whilst much is known, mainly from the *Valor Ecclesiasticus[2]* (*Valor*) and surveys in the records of the Court of Augmentations ('Ministry for Nationalisation of the Monasteries'), about the value of what Henry VIII and his government took, little has been recorded of the area of land involved. However, uniquely useful documents, Abbot Beere's terriers (detailed land records) for Glastonbury Abbey (*circa* 1515-16), have now been traced for 43 of the 57 manors listed in the *Valor* as held by Glastonbury at the Dissolution[3]. Analysis of these and other documents has enabled an estimate of the whole acreage to be made.

1

The exact land holdings of over 2000 tenants have been extracted from the original terriers. Figures for the 14 estates for which Beere's terriers have not been found have been imputed from *Valor* data. Beere and the *Valor* (taken within 20 years of each other) were generally very close and often almost identical. By combining actual and imputed figures, it is estimated that **Glastonbury Abbey owned at least some 130,000 acres** from which it drew an average rent of 4.6d per acre. At today's values (for land with much potential but mostly let on long-term secure tenancies), the **abbey estates would be valued at around £1,500 per acre - say £200 million for the whole.**

Included in the estimates of acreage total are some 7,000 acres of woodland and water along with 23,000 acres of land subject to the common rights of the tenants. The overall information is presented in Table 1 with details in five regional tables (Tables 2, 3, 4, 5 and 6) together with a brief description of each estate.

At the 1086 Domesday survey carried out on the instruction of William the Conqueror, Glastonbury Abbey was shown as holding 1174 hides in Somerset, Dorset, Wiltshire and Berkshire.[4] It is widely accepted that a hide, though a measure for taxation, was nevertheless of the order of 120 acres in Somerset. This would suggest a holding of some 140,000 acres at the time of the conquest. There were of course changes in the intervening years but these do not seem to have been substantial. The last abbot, Richard Whyting in gifting the valuable advowson (the right to appoint a priest to a parish living) of West Monkton church to Thomas Cromwell in a forlorn effort to stave off the destruction of the abbey said that *'in trewth, this was the firste granted out of the monastery as far as I can find knowledge'.*[5] Uplyme in Devon was not included in the 1086 estimate and we know that there were additions and sales after the conquest. However the two estimates are sufficiently close to be of supporting interest.

Analyses of the terriers suggest that some 2,800 tenants depended on the Glastonbury estates for their livelihood. They occupied an average of 46 acres each (including apportioned common grazing rights) and in some cases reed beds, alder groves and other woodland in addition to their houses, which almost always included gardens (probably mainly for food production) and often orchards and little closes of land measured in perches. (Figures for tenant numbers and farm sizes have been imputed for the estates for which no terrier has been found).

These 2,800 working agriculturists supported just 50 monks in the abbey at the Dissolution as well as the administrative bureaucracy undoubtedly in place to manage the abbey assets.

The estate averages are noticeably affected by the inclusion of the major grazing areas of Sedgemoor, *Hethemore* (now Shapwick and Catcott Heath), Godney moor and others, over which tenants had right of common. Overall these comprised between 10,000 and 15,000 acres. Without these extensive grazings, average rents would have been 1d per acre (20%) higher on an area only 8% less.

A hint of the overall estate economy is provided by references in the terriers to wind, water and horse mills (mainly if not entirely for grinding corn), fulling mills (for cloth working), cloth racks and wool washing, to blacksmiths and to coal for smithing, to lime and clay pits, fisheries, dovecotes, apple orchards, salt pans, stone quarries, bee-keeping (for honey and mead), brewing, baking and occupations associated with the use of timber and woodland.

The overall picture is one of tightly, well organised communities working within time honoured but sometimes onerous rules with human nature little different from today. It was a money economy; the monks no longer farmed their land (apart from admittedly substantial areas in the vicinity of the abbey). They took cash in lieu of work duties and tributes.

The customary tenants, who made up by far the largest section of the monastic economy, did not have an easy time. They lived in what would now be regarded as miserable hovels with nothing that would pass today as a window. Their daily workload, on often scant food, would be impossible to contemplate by present day standards. However it is possible to imagine some pleasure in their lives, say in the late spring, with bees at work on the apple blossom in their little orchards, hens starting to lay and cattle and sheep improving in condition after winter hardships. There would also always be atleast the hope of a good harvest ahead with great satisfaction should this prove to be the case.

The lives of the Abbot and 50 monks, the round of abbey services and the politics of the King's divorce and split with Rome will hardly have concerned these men of the soil and they will have adapted with little upheaval to their new masters (or to the same masters under a different authority) after the dispersal of the abbey's massive assets.

As to the monks themselves, two, Roger Jacob and John Thorne perished, executed with their abbot. They were the Treasurers and were considered to be implicated in the concealment of abbey wealth. The remaining monks received pensions and no doubt most found a niche in the secular world into which they had been pitched.

4

Chapter 1   The Wealth of the Abbey

The greatest part of the abbey's wealth lay in the estates which are described in this book. The rental income from tenanted land alone was of the order of £2,750 according to Abbott Beere's surveyors in 1515-16. The King's Commissioners for the *Valor Ecclesiasticus*, 20 years later, fixed the gross income at £3,508 13s 5d for both 'temporal' and 'spiritual' income in 1535 but this was net of management expenses and direct liabilities. These outgoings were mainly for charitable giving fixed at the time of and as a condition of the gift to the abbey. 'Temporal' income came directly from property rents and related manorial income such as fines imposed by the manorial courts. 'Spiritual' income was derived from tithes, the ownership of rectories, parsonages and from alms received. (This latter amount was relatively small at Glastonbury). Alms given, as recorded in the *Valor,* were £140 16s 8d to '*divers poor people as ordained by the foundation and divers founders including King Arthur, the first Christian king; Kenwalchi, Kentwine and Henry VII, Queen Guinevere and Ider, princes Edgar, Athelwolf, Athelbard and Etheldrede and other royals and benefactors as shown to the Kynge's commissioners'.*

A further survey carried out at the suppression by the King's Surveyors, Richard Pollard and Thomas Moyle, of whom more later, produced a much higher figure of £4,224 0s 1d[6]. This was due to woodland and fishing income being included. Woodland and individual trees were also valued, at £4,800 (about £1.4 million today). See page 20. Rental values were also put on land and buildings previously in hand for the benefit of the abbot and convent. These items were generally absent from Beere's survey. Also, Pollard & Moyle excluded many direct liabilities. Twenty years purchase on the *Valor* figure of £3,509 gives some £70,000, perhaps £21 million in today's money. Land in England has increased in value much faster than the rate of inflation since 1535 as the current open market value of the Glastonbury estates would be of the order of £1,500 per acre - say £200 million.

There is no record of the full amount of the non-landed wealth of the abbey but an idea of the amounts has come down to us.

The organising power behind the dissolution of the monasteries was the King's Chief Minister, Thomas Cromwell, who was also made Vicar General to give him a quasi-legal position from which to organise and authorise the monastic suppression and destruction. From 1533 to the first half of 1540, he was one of the most powerful men in the realm but fell rapidly from power and was crudely executed in the Tower of London on July 23rd 1540.[7] His agents were already collecting (stealing) valuables from West Country monasteries early in 1539 but the aged Abbot Whyting at Glastonbury held out against this and it was to be his downfall, as the only indictment against him (for which he lost his life) was that he concealed or stole treasure of his abbey. On October 17th, Pollard & Moyle sent plate (not valued) to London noting *'the total since the last 'sigment* (consignment*) 2,460 ounces'.* [8]   Thomas Cromwell's own notes stated that *'the wealth from Glastonbury that came into the King's hands this autumn was 11,000 ounces beside golden, furniture in ready money £1,100 and rich copes and the years revenues'.*[9] On October 24th 71 ounces of gold with precious stones, 7,214 ounces of gold plate and 6,387 ounces of silver were dispatched from the abbey to London [10]. The execution (many say judicial murder) of the abbot took place on November 15th.   The following day Pollard wrote to

Cromwell stating that even at his death, Abbot Whyting *'would confess to no more gold'*.

There is, however, some circumstantial evidence from over 100 years later[11] that Glastonbury gold had been hidden. *'Where the Porters lodge of the abbey once was is now a good habitable house the Master of which about 30 yeares since pulled down a Mantle piece of a chimney and laid it out in the Street where it lay severrall yeares, he was in price once to sell it asking but ten groats for it but the chapman would give but three shillings. At length his daughter being to build a little chamber, shee got a workman to cut it out to make staires, he trying the stone to see if it were sound found a hole wherein was above fourscore pieces of gold of severall bignesses, the woman got 70 pieces and shee told me the mason kept many more...'*

After November 1539 there seems to have been a hiatus (or lost papers) as the next record found was for June 26th 1540.This noted *'gold and jewels from Glaston and Reading delivered to John Williams, master of the King's Jewels eight items including a super alter called the great Sapphire of Glastonburye delivered May 15th 1540'.*[12] Reading, another Benedictine abbey, was the seventh richest monastic house in England with an income of just less than £2,000 a year. Abbot Hugh of Faringdon had also been done to death on Thomas Cromwell's instructions so that the abbey wealth could be obtained through the 'treason' or attainder of the abbot. But - be done by as you did - Cromwell himself survived only eight months after ordering these judicial murders.
He had made too many enemies and the King held him responsible for the failure of his marriage to Anne of Cleeves.

For comparison, deliveries of treasure shown from other abbeys included Bury St Edmunds: gold (plate?) 1,553 ounces and silver 7,976 ounces; Ely 344 ounces gold and 5,040 ounces silver and Ramsey 16 ounces gold and 2,263 ounces silver.

Further temporal income came from control of the **Manor Courts.** Fines were levied for misdemeanours, often involving trespass or breaches of the peace. The court also extracted entry premiums from incoming tenants. In the *Valor*, the total annual income from these sources was £405 which if capitalised at 20 years purchase would be an asset of £8,100, perhaps £2.4 million today.

The abbey **library** would by today's standards have been of immense value but the surveyors ignored it and the contents were dispersed and / or destroyed.[13] The 'learned antiquary Leland' reported *'how richly it was stored and scarcely equalled by any other library in Britain'.*[14]

The seemingly misnamed **spiritual income** of the abbey came mainly from tithes and advowsons. The *Valor* total was £452 17s 10d for 1535. This, if capitalized at 20 years purchase, would be an asset worth £9,060 - perhaps £2.7 million today.

The annual income assessed as legally due to the King in the *Valor* was £331 2s 9d, less than a tenth of what was obtained from the forced take-over of the assets.

Note: Where money figures have been stated in today's values, a Bank of England guide has been used of £1 in 1535 to be equal to £300 now. Text figures are given in pounds, shillings and pence. 12d = 1shilling. 20shillings = £1.

Chapter 2   Background to the Abbey Estates

General

In the Beere terriers each manor is first described by a perambulation of the bounds (as an example, the entry for Street is given in Appendix A). The jurors, on whose oath the information was confirmed, are also named for each perambulation. Brother Thomas Sutton appears in every one as the Outside Cellarer and he seems to have been the driving force behind the compilation of the whole terrier. 'Estates Bursar' would be a good modern description of his job.   John Horner, bailiff of Mells and steward of the Whitley   Hundred,   was   responsible   for   actual measurements.[15] There were no plans of any abbey property in 1539 - a complete contrast to the present day when a crucial documents in any estate transaction is an accurate estate plan. The boundaries were defined by custom.

It was possible in almost all the terriers to distinguish between arable land, grassland, woodland and water. It was often possible to distinguish between individually held and common grassland and not usually possible to separate meadow from pasture. In the analysis there is, therefore, one figure for grassland, in which is included all houses and buildings. Almost all holdings included a dwelling and curtilage (a little land surrounding it, often accurately measured in perches). Orchards and buildings were commonly referred to, while dovecotes were normally the preserve of the demesne farmer (see page 11). Mills were often noted with an obligation on the customary tenants to use them. Bread ovens and brewing facilities are similarly noted.

9

The *Valor* was undertaken at speed in 1535-6 ostensibly to check the amount of the King's Tithe due to the Exchequer from the whole monastic estate. Underpayment of the tithe may have been widespread and was specifically noted in a margin entry in the Beere terrier for Grittleton in respect of all the Wiltshire manors of the abbey.[16] However it is not clear whether the tax paid was the amount derived from an earlier valuation for Pope Nicholas in 1291. It was certainly a substantially less than 10% of the 1535 rents.

The *Valor* comprised annual rental figures and was not concerned with acreage data. Allowances were made for certain management charges such as bailiff's fees and other outgoings. These have been added back to put the *Valor* figures on the same basis as Beere.

Commons and woods were of major importance to the manorial economy. These are dealt with in following sections. Some areas were specified as woodland but with common grazing beneath the trees. Such areas were taken as common. Fisheries were often noted, in rivers, mill leats and lakes. Meare with its extensive water, from which the settlement derived its name, provided the major fishing enterprise as it had for centuries, there being 10 fishermen and three fisheries recorded in the Domesday record.[17]

Apart from Beere and the *Valor*, a third important source of information has been the survey carried out in 1539 at the Dissolution by Thomas Pollard and Richard Moyle (referred to in future as P&M). These two most unpleasant, devious men were employed by the Court of Augmentations. Their survey, not located in full, has been drawn on through Sir William Dugdale's *Monasticon Anglicanum 1616*[18] and new translations of original material by Margaret McGregor.[19] Information has also been obtained from Abbot Fromond's 14th century terrier.

10

Provenance

Where possible, attempts have been made to show how and when the estates shown in the *Valor* came into the possession of the abbey. Some properties given prior to the Norman Conquest were apparently lost but subsequently regained, particularly through the 12th century efforts of Abbot Henry of Blois, half-brother of King Stephen, papal legatee for England and Bishop of Winchester. Clearly, Henry was a man of influence who used his powers for the benefit of his abbey.

Rental values

Using the Beere data it is possible to estimate relative rental values. Meadow was always the most valuable because the grass could be taken for hay or grazing with little extra work (apart from fencing). Pasture rents were intermediate, with arable lowest, presumably because of the amount of human and ox power needed to get a crop. Typical figures were for meadow upward of 1s 6d per acre, for pasture 7d - 15d, and for arable around 4d. The average for the whole estate was 4.6d per acre (just less then 2p per acre- £6 in today's money). Rents for comparable land now would be ten times this amount showing again how land values and associated rents have outstripped inflation in real terms.

Demesne land

Demesne was land which was or had been 'in hand' i.e. worked by the monks themselves. In later years this ground was let, often as large holdings, by indenture. This deed reflected current terms as opposed to 'customary' terms.

No record of the monks farming their demesne during Beere's abbacy has been found, except for those areas (mainly close to the abbey) held in hand for the personal benefit of the abbot and convent. Land for the abbot's horse (and no doubt his retinue) is noted on several estates. Demesne land was found to be let at rents generally similar to but often a little higher than customary rents. This would be natural as the farmers concerned would tend to be men of competence and capital (otherwise they would be unlikely to gain the tenancies) and therefore willing and able to pay a little more than the average customary tenant. Moreover, the land would probably have been of somewhat higher quality as the abbey might have been expected to get and keep for itself the better land in the days when the demesne was in hand and this would carry through to when it was let. There were some very substantial farmers of demesne land, 300, 400 and 500 acres being recorded to individual farmers. Godney, close to Glastonbury, provided the only example of a manor being almost all demesne and let by indenture. Demesne land in the terriers was noted by an 'O' above the relevant terrier entry and occurred in different situations including customary tenancies in the open fields. Thus demesne land appears to have been fully incorporated into the tenanted estate excepting only the land kept in hand for the personal benefit of the abbot. By 1539, demesne had ceased to have any significance apart from the different form of lease.

Measurement
Some doubt exists as to the actual measure used in Beere for compiling acreages on certain manors. There is little doubt that by this time most land (apart from commons) had been measured out, but wood and arable were sometimes measured by the long perch of 18 feet and meadow and pasture by the short perch of 15 feet. This was the case for Domerham and certain properties close to the abbey. It was not thought practical to undertake meaningful adjustments for this factor but while arable/grass ratios may be distorted, overall totals may not

be greatly affected. In one case, at Othery, the terrier states that holdings were not measured at all but '*indicated by the Jurors as they were in ancyent tymes*'. This may not have been too inaccurate as each tenant would be vying to ensure that he was fairly treated *vis-à-vis* his neighbours.

Acreages held by individual tenants have generally been given to the nearest whole number. Common land has involved major estimation.

Management

Every manor had a bailiff who was normally also a tenant, either customary or demesne. The bailiffs' names and their fees are listed in Appendix C. Fees were an allowable deduction from the amount upon which the King's Tithe was calculated in the *Valor*. Overall, the bailiffs' charges averaged 2.6% of the gross rental. There were also central charges made by the abbey's steward, William Portman, of £10 per annum and the auditors, William Walton, William Hambrigge and John Walton, of £27 0s 6d. Total management and audit charges for a rent roll of some £2,750 were £114 or 4.1 % of the total, very similar to the charges made by land agents today. On secular estates, there were often reeves and bailiffs who reported to a steward.[20] At Glastonbury, it seems that the bailiffs reported directly to the abbey staff. In the time of Abbot Beere, the key man was probably the Estates Bursar/Outside Cellarer, Brother Thomas Sutton. The impression is given that little would have escaped his eagle eye. Entry premiums (fines) were shown against most of the terrier entries but these bore little relationship to the land areas. The income from these premiums obviously varied greatly from year to year and figures for many manors are rounded in the *Valor*. This might be because a deal was struck between the incomer and the estate or that the *Valor* Commissioners, being in a hurry, took the line "Come on, bailiff, gives us your best estimate for an average year, we have to get on". In fact, the *Valor* shows income from entry premiums of £254. This represents about 10% of the rents of £2,750 - a useful extra source of income for the abbey but on average, not too heavy a burden for a young man setting out to make his life on a customary holding.

The *Valor* lists 56 bailiffs, some with double appointments. A few individuals can be identified both as bailiff and tenant in 1515 and still bailiff in the *Valor* 20 years later. Men of differing social standing could hold the position. Edward Bristowe of Grittleton was a half-virgator on some four acres in Beere's terrier as well as being one of the jurors for the perambulation, seemingly as bailiff. In the *Valor*, 20 years later, he still held the office of bailiff. Paul Crasse of Nettleton, villein, held 86 acres and was bailiff in Beere and the *Valor*. John Beks of Wrington also held office over the 20 years. John Horner, a leading land agent for the whole estate, was also bailiff and tenant at Mells. Conflicts of interest obviously arose but there were mechanisms for adjudicating these at the manor courts.

These manor courts met perhaps three or four times a year with the main business done at 'Hocktide' (Easter) and Michaelmas. The chief activity was usually decisions on fines for straying animals especially where crop damage had occurred. Moral and matrimonial matters were also adjudicated on and the bailiff could be called to account for alleged misdemeanours if the customary tenants had the courage so to do. (Free men were not normally required to attend the court).[21]

Status of tenants
The terriers for most estates start by naming a few free tenants owing feudal dues (residual knight/military service) rather than rents. Land areas rented from the

abbey by these tenants were insignificant. Demesne tenants, if any, are then shown, followed by the details of the holding of each customary tenant. No correlation could be found between the ancient status descriptions of ferdellar, half-ferdellar, five-acre man, virgator, etc., specified in the terriers and the amount of land actually held. Even in those cases where the tenant is still described as the lord's villein *(nativus domini)* there is no greater burden of rent or labour service apparent from the record, nor any noticeable difference in the amount of land held.

Layout of holdings

Each entry shown in the terriers listed all the separate areas of land held by each tenant. These have been totalled and entered against each name. A holding normally comprised a number of small strips scattered through the different open fields. Exceptions were large-scale farmers of the demesne who were often noted as holding land in severalty which, confusingly, meant held (and often fenced) individually in separate enclosures, a situation resulting from earlier consolidation and enclosure by the abbey. Details of a fairly typical customary holding (that for Henry Kyngdon at Baltonsborough) are given in Appendix B and a reproduction of the Meare entry for John Grey of Westry is shown as an illustration.

The average size of holding has been calculated by adding grass, arable and common and dividing by the number of individual names appearing in the relevant terrier. However, tenants' rights on commons were not automatically related to the area of the rest of their holding.[22]

Missing manors and imputation of areas and tenant numbers

Beere terriers have not been traced for 14 large and two minor manors listed in the *Valor*. These are Longbridge & Monkton Deverill, Pilton, Batcombe, Ditcheat, Butleigh, East Pennard (see below), West Monkton, (Sturminster) Newton, Buckland, Marnehull, Byndon, Bradleigh, West Stoke, West Coker and, in Monmouth, Barslake. Data for these manors has been imputed on the basis that Beere and *Valor* are close enough to justify this. Indicative figures for 17 mid-Somerset manors which appeared in both records show Beere rents averaging 6.1d per acre and the *Valor* 6.2d. (see Table 4A, page 46). The imputed data has been calculated from agriculturally comparable estates. Dugdale's *Monasticon Anglicanum* refers to *Nylonde* (£13 12s 4d annual value) and *Clewer* (14s 10d). These do not appear in the *Valor* but may be included with other manors. A separate Beere terrier has not been located for East Pennard but it seems likely that the *Valor* entry for West Pennard includes East Pennard, which is also listed separately in the *Valor*. The analysis has been done accordingly.

Crops and livestock

Wheat, oats, barley, rye, peas, vetches and beans were all grown by abbey tenants in the 14th century[23], but cropping obviously differed according to soil type. Livestock noted were horses, cattle, sheep, pigs, doves and poultry. Horses would be used for fast, lighter work especially transport, oxen for the steady pull of ploughing and other heavy fieldwork. The small manor of Wythies (today Withy Farm in the Huntspill levels) is interesting as having been a stud farm for producing oxen in the 13th century and perhaps later.[24] As would be expected, references to sheep predominated on the open chalk downland manors in Wiltshire. Beere and the *Valor* are both silent on farming

16

practices. However it may not be unreasonable to assume that, apart from the cessation of direct demesne management, crop and animal husbandry did not greatly change from the 14th century through to the Dissolution.

Fencing would have been an ever-present problem. Hedgebote (the right and duty to take material, particularly thorns, to repair and maintain fences) is noted on very many manors. There are frequent references, especially in the Polden manors, to the right to 'drove' cattle on the grazing moors/marshes – this, and grazing on self-sown forage on the fallow fields, would have involved constant supervision of the browsing beasts. This was a job often delegated to children. As the old rhyme has it, *'Little boy blue come blow your horn, sheeps in the meadow and cows in the corn'* - everyone come and help get the stock out of the crops.

The urban estate
Although not mentioned in Beere, the *Valor* shows that the abbey held property in London with a gross annual value of £31 17s 7d, and net of sundry pensions, alms and rents, £21 2s 7d. In Bristol a gross rental of £5 13s 4d (£5 net of the bailiff's fee) is recorded. Part of the London property was kept for the exclusive use of the abbot and retinue when on business there. This was valued at £3 6s 8d[25] - seemingly modest accommodation for a major prelate like the Abbot of Glastonbury.

Chapter 3   Woodlands

Timber was a vital part of the economy of most landed estates right up to the beginning of the last century. In monastic times, wood was required and allocated for housebote, firebote, ploughbote, cartbote, hedgebote, foldbote and so on. 'Bote' was the right and requirement for manorial tenants to take material for their own use and for the repair of landlord's property.

Because of its major importance for estate management purposes, woodland was generally kept in hand and (apart from small copses, particularly alder) not let. By its nature, woodland produces a substantial income on felling and to a lesser extent on coppicing or pollarding. Mature woods would have had a high capital value resulting perhaps from 50 or 100 years' growth. Coppice woodland is managed differently and this form of management was very important in earlier years. The 'stools' were coppiced (i.e. cut back to the stump) say every 5, 10 or 15 years depending on the species and need. Coppice woodlands thus provided a regular annual supply of young wood for estate purposes or sale. Income from such woods is often referred to in Glastonbury records. Woodland therefore produced both a regular annual income from coppice re-growth and major capital receipts from mature woods. The most valuable woodland traced on all monastic estates was Wirral Park, in Glastonbury itself, where 60 acres were valued at £4 16s (now £1,440) per acre.[26] This is extremely high and may be an error but excellent mature timber was very valuable.

Abbot Beere's terrier did not cover the estate woods in particular detail as they were managed by the relevant bailiffs and obedientary monks, who were therefore familiar with these assets. Collection of woodland rents was not generally relevant. Alders were however frequently referred to within tenancies and this quick-growing species seemed to be more of a farm/fuel crop than a forestry enterprise. Woodland records were found for many manors, some from Beere but mainly from the P&M 1539 survey (see below) and reported either in Dugdale's *Monasticon* or found in the Public Records Office (PRO). *'Bosc' nul'*, is often noted i.e. 'no woods'. It may be supposed that where woodland was not recorded, all the timber, possibly in short supply, was needed by the estate or its tenants with no surplus for sale. Individual trees were frequently valued and were of course owned by the monastery and not the tenant on whose land they were growing. A typical P&M entry was for *Bukelond* (Buckland Newton, Dorset) : *'Also there be growyng in a common called Deely Wood and Fowlpyttes of grete okys iii (3) worth vjs viiid* (6s 8d) *a 'pec, of polled okys to the number of lx (60) worth to be solde ijs* (2s) *and shrubbe okys to the number of lx* (60) *worth...xijd* (12d) *a 'pec'.* 'Great oaks' were therefore worth some £100 each in today's money.

The *Valor* refers to income from woods (generally taken to be coppice) on a number of manors but rarely if ever to the acreage. This was because the purpose of the *Valor* was, ostensibly, to establish annual income on which the King's Tithe could be levied. Capital values were therefore not immediately relevant but rapidly became so in the mind of the King and his advisors. The more comprehensive woodland and timber record is that found in the Suppression Accounts prepared in 1539 by P&M. In his *Monasticon,* Dugdale listed commercial woods and timber from the P&M survey.[27] These surveyors were zealous in their work as they wished to show up any low valuations in the *Valor*. However, only 17 manors were shown in Dugdale as having woodland and poor transcription is suspected of giving rise to what appears to be an underestimate, many manors being lumped together in this translation with no note at all on woods. Translations by McGregor[28] of original material found in the PRO show some Dugdale material to be of uncertain accuracy. McGregor translations have therefore been used in preference to Dugdale wherever possible. The P&M total acreage reported in Dugdale as being '*in the particular boke of survey at this present tyme made fully, doe appear*' has not been located but reasonable estimates can be made when their data is combined with Beere. The tables show wood and water close to 7,000 acres. The Mere at Meare was about 450 acres, [29] and if 550 acres are allowed for other water, a rounded estimate of 6,000 acres of woodland is arrived at. The commonest species were oak, ash, hazel and maple with few references to elm and none to conifers; '*grete okes and fayre timber*' were often referred to, as were '*lopped, polled* (pollarded) and *shrubbed okes*.'

Capital values were generally clearly distinguished from annual values by P&M. Yearly sales from established woodland were defined as those which did not '*mynyshe spoyle nor hurt, but the woods to contynue as they are nowe*'. P&M (Dugdale) make reference to the sporting potential of the estates: '*Games of fesantes*' are referred to at Domerham, '*games of swanes, heronsewes and fesauntes*' at Meare, and deer at Pilton and in the Glastonbury parks of Northwood, Wirrall and Sharpham. [30]

P&M (Dugdale) put a capital value of £4,800 on all '*woodes and tymbre*' (£2,931 on woodland and £1,869 for the standing timber elsewhere on the estates).[31] The Court of Augmentations valued property at 20 years' purchase i.e. capital value to equal 20 times the annual income as standard practice (and still often the case today) for determining the sale price of monastic land. [32]. Twenty years' purchase on a capital value of £2,931 worth of woodland gives an annual value of 2,931 shillings (£146 11s). If 6,000 acres is taken as the best currently available estimate of the area of Glastonbury woodland, an average annual income of 5.8d per acre is obtained. This, not unexpectedly, is in line with income from other land uses (see Rental Values, page 11) as woodland might be planted or cleared in line with local need for wood relative to food. The Domerham woods (page 27) were particularly productive with an annual income of 9d per acre.

The above data puts the average capital value of the woodland at some 10s per acre, a seemingly very low figure and one to be regarded with caution as with some other Dugdale data from P&M. There are many PRO instances where P&M report much higher values. The timber at Wirrall has already been referred to at £4 16 per acre and five woods around Glastonbury totalling 25 acres were valued at £98 3s 4d - £3 18s per acre[33] This woodland produced an annual income of £3 13s 4d, just short of a 4% yield on the capital value. In addition there were some modest pasture rents, around 2d-8d per acre plus the annual incremental value of the main stand of timber. On this basis, woodland would appear to have been a good investment. However this particular report is dated December 5th 1539, by which day the completed P&M survey was to be sent to London. It is written in a hasty and somewhat scrawled hand and should perhaps be regarded with care.

Chapter 4   Common Land

Areas of common land also played a vital part in the economy of most Glastonbury estates. Beere's terrier combined with P&M shows about half the estates with stated existence of common, but it would be wrong to assume that there was no common land on, or available to, the other properties. Estimates of the existence and areas of commons are not precise. No separate rents were charged for the commons, access being as of right for the manorial tenants with the benefit generally included in the rent paid for the main holding. There was therefore no particular need to record these areas accurately and rounded estimates of the boundaries were often the only record.

The commons were for the exclusive use of the manorial tenants except for the Town Moor at Glastonbury, which may have been open to all townspeople. The estimated overall area of common land is some 23,000 acres. However, much of this comprises certain outstandingly large areas, often being recorded in both Beere and P&M as being measured by 'estimation of the circuit'.

The terms under which the commons could be grazed, and otherwise used, were closely regulated by the manor courts. The largest commons were Sedgemoor, *Hethemore* (now Shapwick and Catcott heath*)* and Godney moor, all in the vicinity of the abbey. They probably totalled between 10,000 and 15,000 acres taken together. This broad estimate is based on Beere and P&M (Dugdale) sources and allowing for what seems like some double counting in the latter.

A study of the OS map (scale 1:25,000 approximately 2.5' to the mile with some 250 acres per square) suggests that such an area was quite possible. P&M (Dugdale) refers to a *'fayre common called Glastonbury Moore, the pasture therof ys very fertile and in effect as good as meade* (meadow*) wherin the tenaunts doe common with theire catall at all seasons of the year and it conteyneth in circuit xvi myles'*. [34] This could be taken as 16 sq. miles, i.e. about 10,000 acres.

Another large common noted was at Sturminster Newton; this was some 2,000 acres where tenants had *'common for their catall all tymes of the year'*.[35]

It was not always easy to distinguish between commons and grassland as part of the field system. For chalkland manors, downland has been shown as grassland. Thus while estimates of the balance between grassland and common may be incorrect, the total areas of land are thought to be broadly accurate.

It is not clear from Beere how areas in common use such as tracks, roadways, headlands and verges were dealt with. Only rare references to roadways were found and in these few cases, a small rent was usually noted as payment for the right to use a particular track. These areas could have taken up quite a lot of land, perhaps five per cent overall but not have been recorded. Thus the area of the total estate could be understated by this proportion.

TABLE 1 Estimate of the Income and Extent of the Rural Estates of Glastonbury Abbey 1539

Based on the Terrier of Abbot Beere 1515-16 with data imputed from the *Valor* (1535) where no record of the estate was traced for 1515-16

Location and (No of Estates)	Total Acres	Gross Rental VE	Rental/acre	No of Tenants	Average size of holding
South Wiltshire (4)	16,000	£270	4.0d	154	101 acres
North Wiltshire (7)	14,000	£225	3.9d	206	62 acres
North Somerset (9)	17,000	£384	5.4d	492	31 acres
Mid Somerset (25)	58,000	£1,194	4.9d	1,442	40 acres
Glastonbury and Northlode (2)	8,000	£360	10.8d	103*	n a
South Somerset and Dorset (8)	13,000	£266	5.0d	376	32 acres
Devon (1)	2,500	£26	2.5d	35	71 acres
Monmouth (1)	1,000	£24	5d	38	26 acres
Totals (57 estates)	129,500	£2,749	5.1d	2,840	46 acres

Notes: Figures imputed for 14 estates based on data for 43. Appropriate averages of rents and holding sizes were used to calculate the imputed figures. * Estimate of agricultural tenants.

Chapter 5   Description of Estates

SOUTH WILTSHIRE (Table 2)

These estates were Domerham with Tidpit and Martin, Idmiston, Longbridge Deverill (*Dev'ellangbrigge*) and Monkton Deverill (*Estemonketon*) containing in all some 16,000 acres with an average rent of 4d per acre.

DOMERHAM (Damerham)

Domerham with Martin and Tidpit, situated on the borders of Wiltshire, Hampshire and Dorset, 11 miles south-south-west of Salisbury, was the largest possession of Glastonbury in the early 16th century. Apart from Glastonbury itself, it also returned the highest income to the central treasury - about £150 (but see below).

    The land is open chalk land sloping from Cranbourne Chase to fertile fields in the valley of the Hampshire Avon. King Edmund gave 100 *measures* of land, defined by perambulation, at *Domerhame cum Mertone et Pentryngton* (Pentridge) to his wife Æthelflaeda with the reversion to Glastonbury on her death. A probable date was 940-946. A further 40 measures were added in 949-957. The 'Pentridge' land was later alienated (sold).[36] (For the purpose of this book, 'hides' and 'measures' are taken to be synonymous).

    At the time of Abbot Beere, the property comprised some 8,600 acres. The *Valor* figure of £119 1s 9d gross is almost certainly an error. Beere gives lists of tenants and acreage for Domerham, East and West Martin and Tidputte, the income from which totals £155. Dugdale[37] shows £159 14s 1d. Martin is not mentioned in the *Valor*. If the Beere income for Martin of £29 16s 10d is added to the *Valor* figure of £119 1s 9d, the total is then £148 18s 7d, and it is likely that something like this figure (£150 taken) should have appeared in the *Valor*.

25

THE ESTATES BY REGION   Wiltshire and Berkshire

TABLE 2

	Beere Total Acres	Beere Total Rent £	Rent d/acre	VE rent £	VE/ Beere diff. £	Grass etc House & Buildings acres	Arable Acres	Arable %	Common Acres	Wood & Waters Acres	No of Tenants	Av. Holding Acres
SOUTH WILTSHIRE												
Domerham, E&W Martin and Tidpit.	8597	155	4.3	150.0	-5.0	4124	3786	48%	0	687	80	99
Idmiston	1732	21	2.9	21.40	0.4	1022	710	41%	0	0	15	115
Longbridge Deverill *	4080	68	4.0	68.00	0.0	1986	1987	50%	0	107	41*	97*
Monkton Deverill *	1845	31	4.0	31.00	0.0	905	906	47%	130	50	18*	108*
TOTALS *imputed	16254	275	4	270	-5	8037	7389	47%	130	844	154	100
N. WILTS & BERKS.												
Nettleton	2063	31.6	3.7	31.40	-0.2	546	1443	71%	50	24	36	57
Grittleton	1158	20.55	4.3	21.80	1.3	309	799	69%	50	0	20	58
Christian Malford	2160	48.45	5.4	48.80	0.3	847	938	52%	13	362	50	36
Badbury	1526	29.5	4.6	29.80	0.3	705	821	54%	0	0	18	85
Kington	2723	27.3	2.4	27.25	-0.1	796	1217	52%	310	400	40	58
Winterbourne Monkton	1511	27.1	4.3	27.25	0.1	323	1188	79%	0	0	14	108
Ashbury (Berks.)	2499	39.9	3.8	38.90	-1.0	1010	1208	54%	0	281	28	79
TOTALS	13640	£185	3.2	225.2	40.7	3526	6406	63%	423	786	206	62

The Abbey Barn at Glastonbury. *(Somerset Rural Life Museum)* A similar barn is still in agricultural use at Doulting Manor Farm.

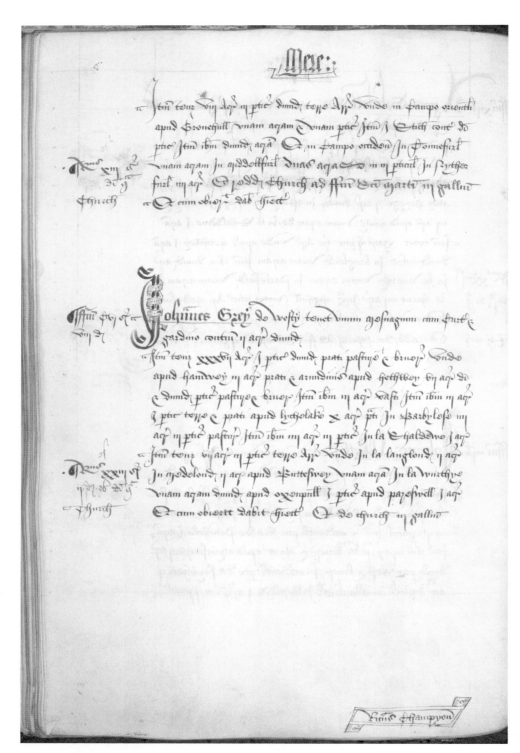

A direct reproduction of a page from Abbot Beere's Terrier for Meare.

Translation of a page from Abbot Beere's 1516 Terrier

(British Library)

Mere

Information from previous entry John Abbot, who held 21 acres with a "Fine" of £4 and rent13 shillings. His entry ends , as most do, with the words:
And when he dies he gives a heriot

Fine   **John Grey of Westy** holds messuage curtilage and
106s 8d   garden containing 2 and a half acres
            -Item he holds 37 acres one and half roods of meadow
pasture and heath
            at Hamwey 3 acres of meadow and reed at Hethwey 7
and half acres
            and half rood of pasture and heath Also in same
place 3 acres waste also 3 acres
            1 rood of arable and meadow at Lychlake 10 acres of
meadow In Barby lese 4
            acres 3 roods of pasture Also same place4 acres 3
roods In La Shaldewe 1 acre
            - Item he holds 7 acres 3 roods arable of which in La
            Langland 2 acres

Rent 23s 2d In medeland 2 acres at Butteswey 1 acre In La
and the   Wurthye
Church
            1 half acre At Oxenpull 1 rood At   Pareswell 1 acre
            And when he dies he gives a heriot and to the
            Church 3 hens

                                        Richard Champion
                                        (Next entry overleaf)

Translation of facing page

A winter view from the Tor looking south-east towards Baltonsborough. (Penny Stokes)
A view probably familiar to the Abbey monks

Average rents overall for this major property were 4.3d per acre and agricultural rents were 5d per acre. The farmland was 48% arable. Average holdings were large at some 99 acres per tenant. Dugdale [38] records extensive timber and woodland while Beere lists seven specific woods. A total of 687 acres has been entered after analysis of both lists. P&M (Dugdale)'s description is of interest: *'dyvers woodes pertaining unto the said manor, very well sett with okes, asshes and maples, the parcells with the acres whereof in the particular boke of survey, at this present tyme made, fully doe appere whiche are estemed now to be worth to be solde over and beside the tymber dxiiii li* (£514). *Also the tymbre growing and being within the saide woodes whereof the nombre of the trees with the several prices in the aforesaide particular boke of survey playnly doe appere is estemed to the value of dlv li xvi s vii d* (£555 16s 8d). *Total of woode and tymbre mlxx li xs* (£1070 10s). *Out of which woodes, the tymbre and olde woodes* (being*) not 'mynyshed, spoyled nor hurt but still to contynew as they are now, there may be a yerely woodsale made thereof to the some and value of xxvi li xd'* (£26 10d - 9d per acre.

The above is quoted at length, partly because it demonstrates the extent of the woodland enterprise at Domerham and partly because sections of the *'boke of survey'* have been located at the PRO and re-translated by Margaret McGregor. The financial totals tie up well as between Dugdale and the new translations. For example, Dugdale's *'Total of wood & tymbre'* amounts to £1,070 0s 7d, while McGregor's *'Summa of saide woodes to be sold out of hand'* of £839 plus the *'Summa of the said underwoddes now redy to be solde yn sundry copsis, great trees reserved'* of £196 16s 8d comes to a total of £1,035 16s 8d compared with the £1,070 7d above, a difference of 3 %.

Sporting rights seemingly had importance on this estate with *'games of fesantes'* and a rabbit warren referred to as being found in the Domerham woods.

IDMISTON (Idmyston)
This chalkland estate lies some six miles north-east of Salisbury with the River Bourne flowing through the valley. In 970, King Edgar granted 10 measures there to widow *Elfswhyt* who had become a nun and later endowed the abbey with her land.[39]
Total area in Beere was some 1,732 acres with one decayed mill noted. There were 1,022 acres of grass and meadow and 710 of arable, 41% of the total. No woods were noted in either Beere or Dugdale. The grass areas were extensive downland including Hayeshill, Rothedown, Comeldown, Holmedown (east of Idmiston, 252 acres) and Wendwexhill (also east of Idmiston, 150 acres) and heathland east of Comeldown (360 acres). No separate rents for this are noted, the value of the common grazing being included in the rents paid by the customary tenants. Total income (adjusted for a double counting error) in Beere was £21 1s - a low figure of 3d per acre accounted for by the extensive thin downland grazings. Fifteen tenants averaged 115 acres apiece, similar to Domerham.

LONGBRIDGE DEVERILL (Dev'ellangbrigge)
No comprehensive terrier has been located. There is no reference in the Great Cartulary, mainly a 14th century document. However, Glastonbury held two estates called *Deurel* in 1066, each of 10 hides. These have been identified as Longbridge Deverill and Monkton Deverill and were probably granted to the abbey by Æthelstan in the 10th century. [40] The estate was some 25 miles east from Glastonbury and 20 miles north-west of Salisbury. The topography is fairly similar to Idmiston and Domerham - chalk with a river valley. If a rent of 4d per acre is imputed

to the adjusted *Valor* income of £68, an area of 4,080 acres is obtained.

MONKTON DEVERILL   (East Monkton)

An incomplete terrier[41] with certain tenancies dated1529 gives an income of £30 14s 6d (*Valor* £30 14s 7d). The area shown is limited to 427 acres of arable, 41 acres of pasture, the total 468 acres shown averaging 5d per acre. There were common grazing rights with allocated stints for specific numbers of sheep on '*Sheepdowne in compace oon myle & half*' (perhaps 90 acres). On Botherdowne '*in compace oon myle*' (perhaps 40 acres), tenants could graze with '*all such other bestes as the holdyng will bere*'. The terrier also notes that whilst woods belong to the manor, the tenants get their timber for repairs from Selwoode within the manor of Deverill. Given the income around the Dissolution of £30 14s and assuming an overall average rent of 4d, then the total estate would have been of the order of 1,845 acres.

SOUTH WILTSHIRE SUMMARY

The four South Wiltshire manors totalled some 16,000 acres with a total *Valor* income of £270, averaging 4d per acre. The land was generally open chalk with fertile river valleys and sheep farming was an important enterprise. Apart from Domerham, woodland income was not significant. The average size of holding was large, at 100 acres and about half arable.

NORTH WILTSHIRE and BERKSHIRE (Table 2)

This group of estates includes the attractive villages of Nettleton, Grittleton, Christian Malford, Badbury, Kington, Winterbourne Monkton and, just in Berkshire, Ashbury, containing in all just short of 14,000 acres. The villages lie mainly along what is now the M4 corridor from Swindon to Chippenham.

As previously noted, the *Valor* was ostensibly carried out to check the King's Tithe, i.e. the 10% tax due on monastic income. Uniquely, the Wiltshire section of Beere carries a specific note of the tithes which were actually paid. These were as follows (Table 2A) with comparisons as to what should have been paid on the basis of 10 % of then current rents:

TABLE 2A	Tithe Under-Payments on Wiltshire Manors 1516		
Manor	Actual Rental from Beere's text	10% Tithe Due	King's Tithe paid
Nettleton	£31 12s	63s	42s
Grittleton	£20 11s	41s	24s
Kington	£27 6s	55s	29s
Christian Malford	£48 9s	97s	60s
Badbury	£29 10s	59s	44s
Winterbourne Monkton	£27 2s	54s	50s
Idmiston	£21 0s	42s	50s
Domerham	£155 0s	310s	225s 6d
Ashbury (Berks)	£39 18s	80s	54s
TOTALS	£400 8s	£40 0s 10d	£28 18s 6d

The note on the tithes actually paid appears in the margin on the Grittleton terrier. Clearly, the abbey was underpaying its tenth on these estates by over 25%, with about £40 being due on these nine manors, instead of the £28 18s 6d actually paid. (The Idmiston figure of tithe paid appears to be a transcription error being identical to Winterbourne above). Underpayment of tithes on the basis of 10 % of current rents may well have been commonplace amongst monastic houses and was one of the reasons why Henry VIII required the *Valor* to be carried out. (Clerical taxation in the early sixteenth century was still based on the assessment made in 1291 by Pope Nicholas IV for his papal tenths).[42]

NETTLETON (Netyleton)

In 944 King Edmund granted 20 measures in Netyleton to his servant Wulfric who later became a monk and brought his charter (title deeds) with him to Glastonbury.[43]

By 1515, there were some 2,063 acres with a high proportion of arable at 71%. Beere records two windmills and a dovecote. Thirty-six tenants averaged 57 acres at an overall rent of 3.7d per acre (4d per acre agricultural only). Thirty-six acres of woods, subject to coppicing every five years, were also noted in Beere, but had reduced to 24 acres of little worth by the survey of 1536 when the surveyors noted *'only an olde house let out by copy'* and a common with no area given (50 acres assumed). [44]

GRITTLETON (Grutelton)

Again, the manor resulted from a grant in 940 by Edmund to Wulfric of 25 measures at *Grutelintone* which Wulfric donated to the abbey on the death of his wife.[45] By 1515, there were 1,158 acres of which *'woodds none but common there of* (blank) *acres'* (50 acres assumed). [46] The arable acreage was also high at 69%. Twenty tenants averaged 58 acres apiece. The demesne land of 275 acres, on which was a dovecote, was farmed out jointly to Messrs Spencer, Calon, Page, Farre & Dun for 118s, an average of 5d per acre, the same as the average agricultural rental for the customary tenants.

CHRISTIAN MALFORD (Christmalford)

In 940 King Edmund granted 20 measures to Dunstan, Abbot of Glastonbury. [47] Beere lists 2,160 acres, including 362 acres of oak and ash woods, which is confirmed by P&M, who report also the (manor) house and barn to be very old and let by copy (no rent given).[48] Arable was 52% of the total, with 50 tenants averaging 36 acres. The average rent of 5.4d per acre and the agricultural rent of 7d suggests good land off the hills.[49] The Beere and *Valor* figures for income are almost identical. Forty acres of demesne, shown in Beere as almost all down to grass, were let to Thomas Stock for 47s 9d which, at 14d per acre, gives an indication of rental values for grassland.

BADBURY

Badbury lies on the north slope of the Ridge Way, south-east of Swindon where King Eadred sold 25 measures of land to Glastonbury for 150 gold shillings in 955.[50] Beere shows 1,526 acres, about half of which was arable. Eighteen tenants averaged 85 acres apiece but only 60 acres if the large demesne farm is excluded (see below); no woods are noted. The *Valor* and Beere incomes are virtually identical with overall rents of 4.6d per acre. Large farmed demesnes were a characteristic of these Wiltshire manors and at Badbury, John More farmed 479 acres of demesne for a rent of £12 3s 4d, i.e. 6d per acre against 4.6d for the average customary agricultural rent.

KINGTON (Kyngetone)

In 987 King Æthelred the Unready, King of Wessex, granted 40 measures of land in *Kynegtone* to Glastonbury valued at 40 pieces of pure gold.[51]

Beere shows 2,723 acres of which 2,014 were agricultural, 52% being arable. Overall rents are very low at 2.4d per acre, but 310 acres of common and 400 acres of wood are shown, 25 acres of the latter being coppiced each year. Agricultural rents averaged 3.25d per acre. The *Valor* and Beere income data are identical. Fourty tenants averaged 68 acres each. Richard Snell (also bailiff) farmed the 212 acre demesne, (60% arable), with extensive buildings and dovecote for a rent of 67s 8d, i.e. 7.6d per acre, there being no hill land to bring the average down. The manor house was, *'fayre with 5 or 6 chambers therein...with two with wene skot* (wainscott) *and horne wyndows ... glased, with buttry, pantry, kechyn, a stable very fayre and the house on one side enclosed with stone'.* [52]

WINTERBOURNE MONKTON

Another Saxon grant by King Æthelred, of 25 hides in 869, apparently gave rise to this manor.[53] Beere shows 1,511 acres, 79% of which was arable, and is in close agreement with the *Valor* on income and overall rents at 4.3d per acre. Fourteen tenants averaged 108 acres, a high figure comparable to the South Wiltshire estates. A major farmer, John Dyverice, held 549 acres of which 94% was arable, and he enjoyed a 'courtly' residence and extensive buildings including *boveria* (cattle sheds). His rent was £12, with common rights on the 255 acre Hakepenne Hill, an average 5.2d per acre overall. A windmill was noted.

ASHBURY (Asshbury), **Berks**

In 947 King Eadred granted to Eadric 20 measures of land. Eadric subsequently passed this land and charter to Dunstan, Abbot of Glastonbury.[54] Beere shows 2,499 acres, about half of which was arable. Woodland of 281 acres is listed, but only 200 acres of wood are noted by P&M. There were common rights in the woods when these were not coppiced (livestock would nibble off the new growth from the coppice stools). The *Valor* and Beere are close on income with Beere higher by £1 at £39 18s. Overall rents average 3.8d per acre including hill pasture rights, with agricultural rents at 4d. Twenty-eight tenants averaged 79 acres each. A substantial farmer of the demesne, Clement North (alias Hardyng), held 476 acres (plus hill pasture for 400 sheep) of which 415 acres (87%) was arable, for £12 6s 8d per annum, i.e. 6d per acre excluding the hill land. In Beere, the manor house was reserved for the use of the abbot of Glastonbury and Oxford scholars, but 20 years later, P&M describe a very fair stone house with chimneys, inner chambers, all domestic offices worth to be let yearly for 13s 4d. [55]

NORTH WILTS and BERKS SUMMARY

This was a homogeneous block of some 14,000 acres, about two thirds arable with an average of 62 acres per holding. The seven manors were in Glastonbury's possession well before the Norman Conquest. The estates were notable for several very large farmed demesne holdings. Average rents overall were close to 4d per acre with the rents of demesne land being a little higher than the customary rents.

34

NORTH SOMERSET (Table 3)

Glastonbury manors taken to be in north Somerset are Lympsham, East and South Brent, Berrow, Wrington, Marksbury with Hunstrete, Camley, Nunney and Mells. The first four comprised a particularly close knit and productive area of some 7,700 acres grouped around Brent Knoll. Altogether, these manors covered about 17,000 acres.

LYMPSHAM (Lymplsham)

Lympsham was in Glastonbury's hands by 1305 in the time of Abbot Geoffrey Fromond (1303-22) but is not listed in the Great Cartulary as a manor. Beere shows 1,656 acres, mainly of grass with only 30% arable. Average rents were high at 7d per acre presumably due to the large proportion of productive pasture. Forty-five tenants averaged 37 acres each. P&M (McGregor) recorded 121 acres of woodland but Dugdale is very brief and uninformative on all these north-western manors. Honey was an important product both here and at East and South Brent; both free and customary tenants had considerable responsibilities for supplying the *medarius* (honey monk) of Glastonbury with stated gallonages of honey or 7d per gallon in lieu. Honey for making mead and as a dietary sweetener was an important element in the domestic life of the monastery. Domerham was the only other manor where the interests of the *medarius* were noted. Millstone rents were common at 4d per customary tenant, as were plough service and haycart service; these latter seem normally to have been commuted for cash. The *Valor* shows a total income of £51 11s and Beere £48 16s. However, it is possible that the *Valor* figure includes services and even honey which were not included in Beere and which could explain the difference.

NORTH SOMERSET

TABLE 3	Beere Total Acres	Beere Total Rent £	Rent d/acre	VE rent £	VE/ Beere diff. £	Grass etc House & Buildings acres	Arable Acres	Arable %	Common Acres	Wood & Waters Acres	No of Tenants	Av. Holding Acres
NORTH SOMERSET												
Lympsham	1656	48.8	7.1	£51.55	2.8	1166	490	30%	0	0	45	37
East Brent	2343	74.1	7.6	£74.30	0.2	1743	600	26%	0	0	101	23
South Brent	2177	52	5.7	£54.35	2.4	1466	570	28%	0	141	78	26
Berrow	1701	41.9	5.9	£43.05	1.2	1080	621	37%	0	0	56	30
Wrington	4404	77.05	4.2	£83.15	6.1	3251	532	13%	400	221	113	37
Marksbury & Hunstrete	1502	25.45	4.1	£24.90	-0.6	278	918	68%	160	146	25	54
Cameley (net of Byconnel)	545	£10.30	4.5	£10.30	0.0	412	0	0%	0	133	6	69
Mells	2291	£37.35	3.9	£42.70	5.4	865	533	38%	0	893	68	21
Nunney	297	£8.45	6.8	£8.45	0	60	148	71%	0	89	20	10
TOTALS	16916	£375	5.3	£392.75	18	10321	4412	26%	560	1534	512	33

Note: Commons, woods and water included in estate totals.

EAST BRENT (Estebrent)

The first indication of Glastonbury's interest in the area of Brent is a charter of 663 in which Ine, King of Wessex, is said to have granted 10 measures of land to Abbot Hæmgils of Glastonbury. The boundaries of this gift were said to be the rivers Severn, Axe and Siger to the south.[56] (The course of the Siger, silted up in medieval times, is thought to have been south of Brent Knoll).[57] After a short period in the late 12th century when it was seized by Savaric, Bishop of Wells, East Brent was back in Glastonbury's hands by 1203 and the Great Cartulary makes reference to maintaining fortifications on 'the Hill' *circa* 1250. [58]

Beere records 2,343 acres of which 1,743 were grass and 600 arable (26%). The *Valor* and Beere give similar income figures, around £74. Rents were again generally high at 7.6d per acre due to the predominance of good grass and there were no major commons or woods noted to reduce the average. One hundred and one tenants held an average of 23 acres each. There must have been some open common land, if only on the Knoll, so the average rent figures must be viewed with caution. Beere records some low rents with high entry fines paid - possibly an attempt to increase current income in the face of an uncertain future.

A manor house is noted in Beere with high rooms and, amongst other appurtenances, a chapel, stabling with an upper floor, and an orchard with fruit worth 40s yearly; no tenant or rent is noted so this may have been reserved for the abbot or other monks and officers of the abbey. There is an unusual record of five shops with upper rooms, rented out at 13s 4d per annum. The interests of the *medarius* again occur frequently, for example, John Gyles pays 17s for his house, yard and 42 acres (4.8d per acre) but in addition must pay to the *medarius* (in whose name the relevant land is held) 2s 6d or five gallons of honey.

Two windmills are noted as are a weir and fishpond let for 3s 4d.

SOUTH BRENT

Also known as Brent Marsh and south-west of Brent Knoll, the origins of the manor are inextricably associated with those relating to East Brent and Lympsham.[59] The Beere terrier records 2,177 acres of which 28% were of arable. Average rents were 5.7d per acre. The *Valor* income was £54 7s, while Beere totals £52 which may not, however, include income such as from honey included in the *Valor*. The Beere survey lists 78 tenants having an average holding of 26 acres and the use of one windmill. There was a lias (blue limestone) quarry here and honey and millstone rents were again much in evidence. There is also reference to cowsheds and dairying, presumably based on the lush meadows of the marsh. Rather surprisingly, no references were found for cheese supplies to the abbey; presumably it was all sold for cash. One windmill was noted.

BERROW (Berghes)

Glastonbury interests in this manor, which adjoins the seashore, were noted in 1310 [60] but it may have been part of the Glastonbury estate as early as the eighth century.[61] Beere shows 1,701 acres (including recent reclamation from the sea) of which 37% was arable. The recorded income was £41 18s, close to the *Valor's* £43 1s. Rents averaged 5.9d per acre. Fifty-six tenants had an average holding of 30 acres. One windmill was noted but no commons or woods.

As for the three preceding estates, there are notes on services due and the cash commutation thereof. Also the majority of Berrow tenants paid annually 3d towards sea wall repairs. There is a long text in Beere concerning a dispute over saltpan rights between Glastonbury and other lordships but no major areas of land were involved.

WRINGTON

The first record of this manor is from 904 and confirms a grant of 20 measures of land at Wrington whereby King Edward the Elder apparently renewed a charter destroyed by fire. According to this charter, Edward granted the land to Æthelfrith who later gave it to his son, Æthelestan, who became a monk at Glastonbury in 957 bringing his inheritance with him. [62]

The estate of 4,404 acres makes this one of the larger manors, situated mainly on land sloping down to the Yeo valley. The land was mostly grass with arable only amounting to 13% of the total. There were 113 tenants with an average holding of 37 acres. The 221 acres of woodland were managed commercially and annual sales were carefully documented. The income from this asset as recorded in Beere amounted to 76s per annum (some 4d per acre) while P&M put it at 100s (5.4d per acre) - slightly above the estate average of 4.8d and the agricultural average of 5d. The surveyors also record '*a common there, called Blackemoore and Warmeshawre whereof...the kyng... hath the profitts of the dryvyng* (droving) *thereof and conteyneth 1 myle dim'*, taken as 400 acres. [63] There were 72 acres of land in hand, some of which was specifically set aside for '*the Abbot's horse';* no rents are shown for this land.

Beere describes a very handsome manor house with ramparts, high walls and deep lakes along with *bartons*, *boveria* and *pinfold* (farmyards, cattle sheds and pound). The pound was maintained by the manor and straying beasts would have been impounded there until the appropriate fine was paid, along with the cost of feed. The *Valor* gives £83 3s as the total income compared to Beere's £77 1s. If the 'in hand' manor house were valued at 15s per annum and the retained land at 5d per acre, then the Beere value would have been £80 1s, closer to the *Valor*. There are extensive references to payments for brewing, pannage (pig feed) and maltings. Cloth making was noted and there were four fulling mills and a 'rack' for stretching the cloth. There were two water mills for corn grinding and a quarry. Development values were also appreciated - John Lovell held a plot suitable for a new watermill and paid 1s a year for it.

MARKSBURY and HUNSTRETE (Merksbury and Houndstrete)
Some three to four miles south of Keynsham and close to the Somerset Wansdyke, these manors taken together comprised some 1,500 acres. Marksbury may have been gifted to the abbey sometime after 926 by one Æthelhelm but this is uncertain and both manors may have been later acquisitions during the reign of King Edgar (959-75). [64].
. The abbey's interests in the area were confirmed around 1157, when Lewyn, son of Ailric of Bristol and chamberlain to the Earl of Gloucester, held land from the monks of Glastonbury for a rent of 10 salmon annually or an equivalent value of 5s.[65] In 1305 Geoffrey Fromond, Abbot of Glastonbury, seemingly instructed John of Yeovil (a practising land agent) to purchase further land adjoining the existing estates.[66]
Beere notes a '*small and beautiful manor house'* built by John Chynock, Abbot of Glastonbury (1375-1420). With the manor house, there was a chapel, courtyard, stables and other *necessary* buildings and orchard all on 1.5 acres. John Chynock was Abbot of Glastonbury for 45 years. He rebuilt the cloister, dormitory and frater (refectory) and finished the great hall and chapter house started by Abbot Fromond.[67]

Beere shows 1,502 acres of which 1,196 acres farmland with arable constituting 68%. P&M recorded 146 acres of wood with commons taken as 160 acres. Twenty-five tenants averaged 54 acres apiece including common. The total income in Beere was £25 9s, in the *Valor* £24 18s. The overall average rent was 4.1d per acre and agricultural rent 4.8d per acre. One water mill was noted

Within these totals, demesne land of 323 acres was farmed in some style by Nicholas DeTell at a rent of 6.5d per acre. The demesne arable to grass percentage was similar to the customary at 72% arable. DeTell was therefore paying rather more per acre than the customary tenants. If however, he was a superior husbandman, a higher rent would be understandable and, as elsewhere, former demesne land was likely to be better than average quality. Abbot Fromond's terrier of *circa* 1316 [68](before the population was massively reduced by the Black Death in the 1340s) showed demesne arable land let at 8.3d per acre and a total demesne of 240 acres grass and arable let for an average of 10.8d per acre. Rents here seem to have been noticeably higher in the early 1300s than 200 years later.

CAMELEY   (Camleigh)
Cameley lies two miles north-north-west of Midsomer Norton and came to Glastonbury as part of a donation by Sir John Byconnel (date not traced). The manor comprised some 1,364 acres at the time of the Beere terrier but was burdened with a number of charges, in particular £33 6s 8d per year for the support of 10 students at Oxford.[69] The gross value in Beere was some £21 14s with overall average rent at 3.8d per acre and agricultural rents at 4d per acre on average; demesne rents were 5d per acre. Beere does not refer to the charges on the manor but the net *Valor* figure is only £10 6s. There is, however, a major discrepancy as the *Valor* implies a gross value of £10 6s plus the Oxford students' charge of £33 6s 8d making some £43 13s in all, about twice the Beere figure. No

information was found which might suggest which figure was right, but clearly the whole interest cannot be regarded as belonging to Glastonbury. The abbey's residual income was £10 6s (see above) or, say, the revenue from about 500 acres and, therefore, the Glastonbury interest was probably effectively limited to 5-600 acres. There were six tenants with an average of 69 acres each. P&M note that '*The Kynges Majestie hath woodes there*', totalling 133 acres.[70] An estimate of 633 acres has been taken for Glastonbury's interest in the property.

NUNNEY
This was a small manor of some 297 acres. The village is dominated by the splendid moated castle and most land in the area no doubt attached thereto. Glastonbury, according to Beere, had 20 tenants averaging only 10 acres each. Rents were 6.8d per acre, possibly reflecting the high relative value of a dwelling on a small holding. Nunney appears in Beere and P&M but not in the *Valor*. This would seem an oversight in the *Valor*.

MELLS   (Mellez)
Edmund, King of the English, granted to his 'faithful Earl', Æthelstan 20 measures of land at *Milne* (Mells) in 942. This may be the same Æthelstan who became a monk at Glastonbury and took his charters for both Mells and Wrington with him. Glastonbury was confirmed as overlord in 1253.[71] Abbot Beere's terrier suggests that the manor comprised 2,291 acres of which only 533 acres were of arable (22%), 865 acres of grassland and a very high proportion of woodland and scrub (893 acres) at 38% of the total. The overall average rent was 3.9d per acre and the agricultural land was rented at 6.6d per acre. Beere gives an income of £37 7s and the *Valor* £42 14s. P&M recorded only 100 acres of woodland proper, 60 acres being managed on a 20-year coppice rotation while 40

acres were reserved for the tenants' use. Hedgerow elms are noted, being aged 40 years or more and worth an estimated two shillings (£30) each. Timber was also specifically reserved for the repair of property in Glastonbury town. Sixty-eight tenants averaged 21 acres each. The bailiff in 1516 was John Horner, drawing an annual fee of 25s. (He was also bailiff of Whitley Hundred and involved quite widely in the management of the monastic estate). Tradition has it that astute intervention secured him or his son the estate at the Dissolution, albeit at a fair market price, whether or not the title deeds were hidden in a pie. John Horner is said to be the original of the nursery rhyme "*Little Jack Horner sat in a corner, eating his pudding and pie. He put in his thumb, pulled out a plum and said 'What a good boy am I' ".* Be all that as it may, the records of the Court of Augmentations show a purchase of property on July 10th 1543, at 22 years purchase by Thomas and John Horner in the sum of £1,831 19s 11d. [72] However, P&M (McGregor) do record in 1539 that '*the parsonage ys in the Kynges gyfte and worth by the yere to farm XXXli* (£30), *the vowson wherof is graunted to Master Horner ut dic'* ('so they say'*).* Perhaps the grant of the parsonage gave rise to the story.

Mells had a thriving woollen industry. There were seven fulling mills, a specialist wool washer and racks for stretching the woven cloth. Stone quarries, coal and lime pits are also recorded. The abbey did not invest in the fulling mills as it is shown as receiving ground rents only. Beere notes three water mills.

NORTH SOMERSET SUMMARY

There were 17,000 acres at an average overall rent of close to 6d per acre. The four north-western estates, centred round Brent Knoll, included major honey, salt and dairying enterprises.

MID SOMERSET TABLE 4

	Beere Total Acres	Beere Total Rent £	Rent d/acre	VE rent £	VE/ Beere diff. £	Grass, Hse & Buildings acres	Arable Acres	Ara ble %	Com'n Acres*	Wood & Waters Acres	No of Tenants	Av. H'ld'ng Acres
Doulting	2506	39.40	3.8	40.75	1.4	904	1177	57%	0	425	47	44
Pilton (imputed)	3874	94.80	6.1	94.80	0.0	1864	1864	50%	0	146	116	32
Batcombe (imputed)	1228	31.20	6.1	31.20	0.0	614	614	50%	0	0	38	32
Ditcheat (imputed)	2268	57.66	6.1	57.66	0.0	1134	1134	50%	0	0	71	32
East Street (by Norwood)	256	10.85	10.2	10.55	-0.3	102	154	60%	0	0	25	10
E&W Pennard +Bradley (imp)	5341	110.60	5.0	107.40	-3.2	1749	1748	35%	1500	0	102	49
Pulle (imputed)	10	0.25	6.1	0.25	0.0	5	5	50%	0	0	2	5
Baltonsborough	4006	89.65	5.4	93.25	3.6	1162	636	20%	1347	861	98	32
Butleigh (imputed)	3064	49.10	3.8	49.10	0.0	965	966	50%	1000	133	70	42
Meare incl. Hethemore	5371	64.50	2.9	56.05	-8.5	1167	347	7%	3300	557	65	74
Godney	2544	43.80	4.1	41.00	-2.8	534	535	29%	750	725	113	16
Shapwick*	3490	57.00	3.9	59.70	2.7	755	1485	43%	1214	36	51	68
Middlezoy*	2570	80.00	7.5	79.00	-1.0	1123	647	25%	800	0	84	31
Weston Zoyland *	3275	91.75	6.7	101.00	9.3	1327	798	24%	1150	0	114	29
Othery*	1955	56.40	6.9	73.75	17.4	674	681	35%	600	0	81	24
Street*	2609	48.50	4.5	47.50	-1.0	665	1064	41%	840	40	44	58
High Ham*	3042	50.75	4.0	50.00	-0.8	429	1491	49%	1100	22	54	56
Walton*	2628	40.75	3.7	42.33	1.6	387	1091	42%	1100	50	51	51
Ashcott*	2306	31.05	3.2	29.40	-1.7	440	1082	48%	750	34	40	57
Greinton*	903	17.30	4.6	19.50	2.2	179	424	47%	300	0	27	33
Moorlinch*and Withy Farm	915	28.30	7.4	15.75	12.5	406	309	34%	200	0	22	42
West Monkton (imputed)	2348	59.70	6.1	59.70	0.0	1174	1174	50%	0	0	73	32
Milton Podimore	784	21.80	6.7	23.20	1.4	397	387	49%	0	0	22	36
TOTALS	57293	1175	5.0	1184	8	18156	19813	47%	15951	3118	1410	38

* denotes common rights on Sedgemoor./Hethemore, 10,000 acres divided pro rata by acreage between the manors

44

MID SOMERSET (Table 4)

This is the largest grouping in the analysis, with 25 manors totalling some 57,000 acres. They include some of the earliest endowments of the monastery. In 702, King Ine of the Saxons is reputed to have given Doulting to Glastonbury and in 729 Athelard, King of the West Saxons, is recorded as having given to the monastery the whole of the Polden Hills (*Poholt/Pouelt*). This area extended approximately from Street to Chedzoy thence to Mudgley and back to Street. [73]

Discrepancies and apparent errors between Beere, the *Valor* and P&M (Dugdale) texts occur in the Mid Somerset estates. Nunney with 296 acres appears in Beere and in Dugdale but not in the *Valor*; this must be an oversight in the *Valor*. West Pennard seems to include East Pennard in the *Valor* but East Pennard is also listed separately in the *Valor* and has been excluded to avoid double counting. Apart from East Pennard, Beere terriers could not be traced for six mid-Somerset manors: Pilton, Batcombe, Bradley, Ditcheat, Butleigh and West Monkton.[74] For the six missing manors, acreages and tenancies have been imputed from the average of the other 17 manors considered comparable (see Table 4A overleaf). The *Valor* average for these 17 is 6.2d per acre and the Beere average 6.1d per acre. These are thought to be close enough to justify the interpolation of the remaining five at 6.2d.

TABLE 4A		Valor & Beere Compared	
Mid Somerset Estates in both Surveys			
Estate	Income £s Beere	Income £s Valor	Acres Beere
Baltonsborough	90	93	2806
Shapwick	57	60	2426
Middlezoy	80	79	1770
Street	48	47	1768
Ham	51	50	2159
Walton	41	42	1908
Ashcott	31	29	1557
Milton	22	23	784
Greyington	17	19	603
Weston Zoyland	92	101	2125
Othery	56	74	1375
Withy	23	16	350
East Street	11	11	256
E&W Pennard	102	99	3497
Meare	64	56	5371
Godney	44	41	2687
Doulting	39	41	2507
Totals	868	881	33949
Av. Rent d/acre	6.1	6.2	

Sedgemoor was a major asset for many of these manors, certainly for those marked with an asterisk in Table 4. P&M indicate the area as 15 miles in circuit, taken for the purpose of this book at 10,000 acres. In order to achieve recognition of this area, it has been divided (*pro rata* to the size of each estate) between those manors in Beere noted as having grazing rights. It is almost certain however that this is not how the grazing rights would have actually been divided.

DOULTING

In June 702, King Ine gave 20 measures of land on either side of the Doulting stream to Abbot Beorwald of Glastonbury, but there is some doubt about the precise location of this land in relation to the neighbouring manor of Pilton (see below). It is however clear that Doulting was an early possession of the abbey. [75]

Beere indicates 2,506 acres with (unusually) substantial amounts of wood and furze included in the tenancies, but *'of other woods none'*. [76] Beere rents amounted to £39 8s and in the *Valor* to £40 15s. The 283 acres of the demesne, including ox house and dovecote, were farmed by John Whyte at a rent of 7.5d per acre. The estate average (excluding woods) was 5d per acre. A four-acre quarry was noted (probably the one which provided the stone for a barn at Street over 200 years earlier as well as for the splendid barn still in agricultural use on Manor Farm. [77] Forty-seven tenants averaged 44 acres each including woods.

PILTON (Pulton)

King Ine may have granted an estate of 20 measures at Pilton to Glastonbury in 705, but the precise area and date of the original grant are bound up with the nearby manor of Doulting. [78]

The data for 1536 has been imputed at 3,728 acres. Abbot Fromond's terrier of 1317 [79] describes a large and wealthy manor with commons, parks, woodland, dovecotes and a watermill. There were then 10 free tenants, 10 tenants for life and 162 customary tenants. Rents were quite as high as some 200 years later with arable consistently at 6d per acre and grassland at 20d. Work services listed in Fromond seemed onerous but had gone by Abbot Beere's time. Woodland with large oak, ash, hazel, maple and thorn is mentioned but not valued. Possibly all woodland products were utilised for estate repairs and maintenance.

Pilton (Pulton) Park is referred to in the *Valor* separately from the manor with an annual value for hay of £2. P&M [80] describe it in great detail and it may have been another property held in hand for the pleasure of the abbot of the time. It had a *'feyr curtilage, walled with a feyr gatehouse, a feyr open hall with hearth, 2 porches, 10 feyr chambers, a long chapell with bellhops, a wyne cellar, a prety pantry & butry, a feyr kitchen & larder, a bakehouse, a woodhouse, a stabull for 10 horses, a fair pichyn house and orchard and garden adjoining the parke of wood and good pasture containing in circuit 3 long miles* (350-400 acres?) *plenysshed with 350 deer and a feyr streme running through the same'*; seemingly a very desirable property. A contiguous document records the value of the herbage of the park as being worth £12 annually (rather than the £2 of the *Valor*) and woodland is detailed at 272 acres within the park. What would Brother Thomas Sutton have made of the Glastonbury festival had he done a perambulation of Pilton in the early 21st century ?

BATCOMBE (Badecombe)
This estate has been imputed at 1,228 acres. Fromond's terrier describes the demesne land fully with rents (it seemed not to be in hand) but does not give clear total acreages for the customary tenants. Meadow, pasture, arable and commons are described along with responsibilities to fence Pilton Park. A watermill and pannage rights are also mentioned.

DITCHEAT

This has been imputed at 2,268 acres. Fromond's 14th century terrier again recorded all the demesne land by type and rent. There was a dovecote, windmill and woodland for estate purposes. The record of customary tenants was insufficient to form a clear idea of the total areas held but names and full details of work services required are shown. P&M state '*Bosc' nul*' - woods none.[81]

EAST STREET (Estrete)

A small manor estimated at 256 acres to the east of Norwood Park, but with at least 25 tenants. The terrier breaks off on a half completed page. However, it does record the farmer of the demesne, Henry Thomas, as holding a house, buildings, dovecote, 60 grassland acres in six fields and two acres of arable at an average rent of 15d per acre (reflecting the high proportion of grass). The customary holdings were small (10 acres average). Possibly incomes were supplemented by work at the abbey close by. Overall rents were high at 10d per acre, again reflecting the value of a house on a small holding.

EAST and WEST PENNARD with 'BRADLEY'.

The first record of this possession is of a gift by King Baldred in 681 of an estate defined in the usual way by a description of the boundaries.[82]

These were separate manors at the dissolution but all clearly owned by Glastonbury. Beere's terrier gives a value for West Pennard of £51 1s with no terrier found for East Pennard. The *Valor* gives West Pennard at £98 17s and East Pennard £51 0s 5d. It is therefore logical to think that the *Valor* commissioners double counted by including East Pennard with West having already correctly entered it under its own name. Taken together, the Pennards totalled some 5,000 acres. Rents averaged 4.9d per acre and 102 tenants averaged 49 acres apiece with 35% arable. The

Beere terrier records only 25 acres of common but P&M record a common of 15 miles in circuit, ie about 9,000 acres, *'wherein all tenants of said manors doe entercomen'*. [83] This area is thought to involve double counting of Sedgemoor and has been excluded though this interpretation is open to doubt. The *Valor* commissioners may have been badly briefed and got in a muddle over the Pennards. The tenants themselves may also have been a difficult lot as Abbot Beere's surveyors note specifically that *'troublesome tenants will lose their tenancies'*. **Bradleigh** (taken to be West Bradley) has a brief entry in the *Valor* showing gross rents of £8 12s, imputed at 344 acres.

PYLLE (Pulle)

Pylle is recorded in Beere as having 31 acres and just one tenant, Thomas Joce, paying an annual rent of 5s. An orchard, a second cottage and a grove of alders were noted. There is no apparent reason for the very low rent of 1.9d per acre.

BALTONSBOROUGH

The first record of Baltonsborough is from 744 when *'Lulla, handmaid of Christ, granted* to *Abbot Tunberht and the monks of Glastonbury ten measures of land... putting the charter on the altar of St. Peter and Paul with her own hand'*. [84]

By 1515 this was a substantial manor occupying some 4,000 acres, lying south of West Pennard with one third of the farmland being arable. There were about 800 acres of wood consisting of *Southwoode* with 420 acres well set with *'okes both olde and younge'*, and *Northwoode*, similarly set. Both woods were 'shred' every 20 years (ie lopped for the value of the branches). P&M give the capital value of these woods as £400, or some 10s per acre. [85] There were 147 acres of common for the exclusive use of the lord's tenants as was normal. A 1,200 acre share of Sedgemoor has been included. An average agricultural rent of 12d per acre was paid by 98 tenants. The average rent for the whole estate was 7d per acre, levels which suggest that this was a fertile and successful manor. The demesne was leased to Walter Cary and comprised a courtyard residence, stables, grange, cowsheds, dovecote and pinfold; in addition Walter enjoyed 85 acres of meadow and pasture in five enclosed fields and eight acres of wood in the demesne. Unusually, no arable was noted. His rent was 1s 10d per acre - reflecting the high proportion of grass.

Beere records the details of a dispute between the tenants of Baltonsborough and neighbouring Butleigh. The former claimed that the latter were guilty of entry and trespass, of de-pasturing the grass, carrying off underwood, thorns and other fuel and harassing the pigs in the wood. The abbot's officials decreed that Baltonsborough men should impede the men of Butleigh to the best of their ability and present the trespass at the next court and exact forfeit. Baltonsborough men went further and said they would *scatter the Butleigh men and make formal immediate notification of their names'*.

BUTLEIGH

Early charters indicate that Egbert, King of the West Saxons, gave his servant Eadgils the occupation of 20 measures at *Buddekauleghe* in 801 and Eadgils then gifted the 20 measures to Glastonbury with the consent of King Egbert. [86]

No Beere terrier has been found but at the Dissolution 1,931 acres of farmland have been imputed at 6.1d per acre, plus 1,133 acres of common including woods of 133 acres. [87] Butleigh common is now shown on the OS map south of Ashcott below Priest Hill and well west of Butleigh village. There were, or rather had been, fisheries: '*There is a severall fysshinges from Tylesco brydge to Cowbrydge the rent whereof was 6s 8d now altogether in decay for as much as the weare was put down by Comysshioners of the Sewers'*. P&M also note a complaint, '*memorandun to advertyce Mr Surveyors how that the King's tenauntes of His Graces manor complayneth that Mr Strangwais, tenaunt of Compton Donden*,(adjoining to the west) *oppresseth the commens of this manor with more cattell than they can keep upon their tenures in wynter....and desire for the reformacon thereof that it will please the said Mr Surveyors to wryte unto the said Mr Straingwais that he may cause a redress...*'.[88]

The Fromond terrier (*circa* 1315) shows land amounting to 747acres of arable averaging 4.7d per acre and 170 acres of meadow and pasture at 1s 6d per acre average. Again, evidence of rents then being atleast as high as 200 years later.

MEARE

The mere dominated this eponymous manor, which may have been a late seventh-century gift to the abbey.[89] Covering about 450 acres it lay to the north of the village and stretched across to what is now Meare Pool Farm at Godney. The abbot's fish house remains in good order and is understood to have been the residence of the steward in charge of the mere, which was drained in the late 16th-early 17th century.[90] Beere gives 1,167 acres of grass and 347 of arable; *Hacchemore* or *Hethemore* (now Shapwick and Catcott Heath) of 3,300 acres and oak, alder and ash wood of 107 acres giving an estate total of 5,371 acres. The residence is described as a large and beautiful manor with fishponds and orchards surrounded by high thick walls. The P&M survey goes into greater detail and refers also to a '*prety house for the fysshers to drink in... and another prety house of stone with a little hall and parlour... orchard, two garden plottes, three ponds and an olde thatched house to cover their fysshing boates ...and a goodly fysshings water being 4 or 5 myles in compasse'*. It was an obviously attractive property which could also have been used socially by the incumbent abbots apart from its propensity to bring on ague or marsh fever, for the surveyors also noted that *'the ayer is not very holesome savyng to suche as have contynued long therein'*. [91]

GODNEY (Godenhay)

Godney was one of the 'islands' of Glastonbury which the abbey claimed to have been gifted to them by King Cenwealh in 642-72. [92] At the Dissolution it comprised some 2,544 acres of which 1,070 acres were farmland, all of which was demesne (let by deed of indenture). The division between grass and arable was not given but assumed to be half and half. P&M show 1,450 acres of common (Godney/Godley Moor) and much *'fayre tymber'*. [93] An incomplete Beere terrier is supplemented by P&M records in the PRO[94] which give details omitted from Dugdale's *Monasticon*. Godney Common, shared with the Dean of Wells, was said to be *'six myles in cyrcute'* (taken to be 1,500 acres and halved to allow for the Dean's interest). It included twelve acres of alders *'felled* (coppiced*) for three years past'*, two acres of oak and willows and 80 standing oaks and 15 ashes reserved for repair work in Glastonbury. Also in the manor was the 33-acre *Brodeoke Common* which included five acres of wood with standing timber also for repairs. Average rents were 4d per acre overall but 8.5d per acre if moorland grazing is excluded. A total of 113 tenants held an average of about 22 acres each. Incomes may have been supplemented from fishing in the mere and work at the abbey. Beere does not show any customary tenants though P&M (Dugdale) show a small customary rental of 17s 10d. Godney was perhaps one of the last places where the abbey farmed in hand for profit. The rents show little difference from customary lettings in the area and this supports the hypothesis that there was little rental difference between customary and demesne lettings. A chapel is recorded but as being *'violated by birds'.*

SHAPWICK

The origins of the Shapwick manor are closely bound up with the history of the Polden (*Pouelt)* estate with its probable donation to the abbey in the 8th century (see the Mid-Somerset summary above). At the time of the Beere terrier, Shapwick had 51 tenants averaging 68 acres with an arable 43% of the total. Rents by land type were noted: arable rents averaged 4d per acre, pasture 10d and meadow 14d, which gives an idea of both relative and absolute values. The total estate was 3,490 acres to include 1,100 acres of Sedgemoor. The terrier also records a common of 114 acres and '*a woode called Lokesleys'* of 36 acres set with oak, ash and thorn (today's Loxley Wood). The tenants shared, with those of Meare, grazing and turbary rights on *Hethemore* on a clearly defined basis and grazing on Sedgemoor shared with other neighbouring manors. A windmill with an annual value of 26s 8d was noted, as was a lias quarry.

ZOY (Sowey)

Although listed separately in Beere, the villages of Middlezoye, Weston Zoye and Othery were taken as one manor (being in effect an island between Sedgemoor and the moors to the south) of about 7,800 acres which figure includes an apportioned area of Sedgemoor. It supported 280 tenants with an average of 28 acres each; the boundaries of the group are given in Beere under Weston Zoyland. This combined manor, probably dating from a charter of King Ine and his wife Æthelburgh in 725, [95] showed the biggest deviation in the whole study between the *Valor* and Beere, with the *Valor* being about 10% higher. No obvious explanation has shown itself but it might be that the extensive 'works' to maintain the flood defences and Greylake Causeway (see below) were valued for cash in the *Valor* but not in Beere. The Causeway, now the A361, was constructed around 1300 to link the island with Glastonbury and tenants had specific duties to repair and maintain this roadway. The rents on all three villages were close to 7d per acre, the high level reflecting the low proportion of arable and absence of thin upland grazing.

MIDDLEZOY (Middelsowye)
Middlezoy comprised 2,570 acres in Beere with 25% arable and 84 tenants averaging 31 acres each. Beere and *Valor* rents were similar at £79-£80. One John Parson worked '*atte quarry*', and there was a windmill and a horse mill; obligations were noted for tenants to use the communal bread oven and to pay tax on the brewing of ale.

WESTON ZOYLAND (Weston)
This was one of the more valuable possessions of the abbey with an annual income of £101 in the *Valor*. It lacked '*woddes and severall* (enclosed) *waters*' [96] but its 3,275 acres (24% arable) plus the 300 acre Weston Common shared with the tenants of Chedzoy (not a Glastonbury manor, a half share therefore being attributed to Glastonbury), were clearly productive with rents close to 7d per acre. There were 114 tenants who averaged 29 acres each. A horse mill was valued at 14s per annum. P&M reported *'a fayr hall, parlar, five chambyers, bottery, pantry, sellar, kechyn……..a fayr dove house…a great chamber without the hall for servantes to lye yn…a great stabele, a lyttle stabell, a bruhouse, a grete barne, a lettyl house to the same…a gardyne enclosed with a wall… bordes, frames and bedsteades yn every house'.* [97] Demesne land included a 15-acre croft adjoining the barn

let at 2s per acre per year and Warde Close of nine acres adjoining and let at 1s 8d per acre.

OTHERY
Beere gives 1,955 acres (with a share of Sedgemoor included) of which 35% were arable. Eighty-one tenants averaged 24 acres each. There is a major discrepancy between Beere and the *Valor*. (see comment page 54-55). Again no woods but a stone quarry is noted. The terrier also states that the fields of Othery were not measured by the '*measureing rod*' but were '*indicated*' by the jurors of the manor as they were in '*ancyent times*'.

STREET
Now an attractive town, the origins of Street as a Glastonbury possession are obscure, but it was possibly part of the donation of *Lantokay* in the late 7th century.[98] In 1536 it was a fairly typical manor of some 2,609 acres with a due proportion of Sedgemoor included. Arable took 41%. The *Valor* shows income of £47.50, Beere £48.50. Rents were close to the overall average at 4.5d per acre and 44 tenants held an average of 58 acres each. There were 840 acres of common (including an 800-acre share of Sedgemoor) and 40 acres of wood. The perambulation of Street is set out in full in Appendix A.

HIGH HAM (Hamme)
This manor, high on the hills some seven miles south-west of Glastonbury and south of Sedgemoor, must have provided an excellent vantage point for much of the abbey property. It came through a grant and land exchange from Edgar, King of England, in 973. [99]

Income at the Dissolution was £50 per annum from 3,042 acres including 900 acres of Sedgemoor. Arable was 49%. Rents averaged 4.0d per acre overall and 54 tenants averaged 56 acres apiece. There were 200 acres of common and 22 acres of wood. Additionally, Beere states that the tenants here had common rights on Sedgemoor along with Walton, Ashcott, Shapwick, Greinton, Moorlinch, Middlezoy, Othery and Weston Zoyland. Apart from grazing, the tenants could dig turves for fires and cut sedge for their own use. William Balch, the farmer of the demesne, was in a fair way of business; he held 236 acres of which 188 were arable and his buildings included a farmyard, granary, ox-house and the pinfold (pound). His rent averaged 4.7d per acre.

WALTON

Walton probably shared a common origin as a Glastonbury possession with Shapwick (see above). An acreage of 2,628 is shown in Beere. The *Valor* rent total was £42 6s (averaging 3.7d per acre) compared with Beere's £40 15s. The area was 61% arable with 300 acres of common and 50 acres of woods. Eight hundred acres have been included as the manor's share of Sedgemoor. Demesne rent on 137 acres averaged 6d per acre. Fifty-one tenants averaged 50 acres each. As well as rights on Sedgemoor, Walton tenants also had rights on *Hethemore.*

ASHCOTT (Aisshcotte)

Ashcott's origins are, like those of Walton and Shapwick, probably to be found in the early grant of the Pouelt estate (see above). Beere records 2,306 acres (to include a 700 acre share of Sedgemoor). The estate was 48% arable. Forty tenants averaged 57 acres apiece. The *Valor* rent total was £29 8s, an average of 3.2d per acre. There were 50 acres of commons and 34 acres of woodland including '*oke, asshe, hasell, maple and thorns, to be felled to the ground* (coppiced) *every twelve or fourteen years,*' but so-called 'great' trees were reserved. [100] The demesne of 184 acres (53% arable) was farmed by William Browning at a rent of 5.3d per acre and he presumably also enjoyed common grazings.

GREINTON (Greyngton)

This modest estate came to Glastonbury in 1290 but whether by purchase or gift is not clear. [101] On the south side of the Polden Hills, it extended into Sedgemoor and was at the northern end of the Greylake Causeway connecting it with the Zoy (Sowey) estate. Beere records 603 acres to which a 300 acre allocation of Sedgemoor has been added. Forty-seven per cent was arable; rents averaged 4.6d per acre and 27 tenants averaged 33 acres apiece. No woods or quarries were recorded by P&M.

MOORLINCH and WITHY (Murelynch and Withies)

In the *Valor* this manor (again with origins in the *Pouelt* estate) is put with Shapwick, Pedwell and Sutton Sowey, in a way which suggests that the Commissioners were not quite sure what was what. Beere shows 394 acres to which have been added 200 acres of Sedgemoor. The total was 52% arable with rents averaging 2.2d per acre. Twelve tenants averaging 50 acres each. A note in Beere states that floods had devastated the manor, hence presumably the very low rents. P&M report *'woodes, quarries and severall waters – nul'*. [102] **Withy Farm *(Wythies)*.** This small sub-manor (in the 14th century it was described as a hamlet of Shapwick) does not appear in the *Great Cartulary* but was in the possession of the abbey by the 13th century, when it was a specialist stud farm for the breeding of oxen [103]. Beere gives 350 acres, all of which were meadow or pasture, and a value of £22 19s, an average of 16d per acre reflecting this unusual composition. There were 10 tenants averaging 35 acres each. No woods are recorded but *'fysshyngs'* were reported in Beere.

The Abbot's Fish House at Meare. (Penny Stokes) F&M noted a
pretty house of stone with a little hall and palour.
The mere lay behind the building.

The Abbot's Kitchen, Glastonbury Abbey, built by Abbot Whiting and the last constuction before the dissolution.

Give me a good digestion, Lord,
And also something to digest
Give me a healthy body, Lord,
With sense to keep it at its best.

Give me a healthy mind, O Lord,
To keep the good and pure in sight
Which seeing wrong is not appalled
But finds a way to put it right.

Give me a mind that is not bored,
That does not whimper,
                    whine or sigh,
Don't let me worry overmuch,
About that fussy thing called 'I'.

Give me a sense of humour, Lord,
Give me the grace to see a joke,
To get some happiness from life
And pass it on to other folk.

An Ancient Prayer from Glastonbury Abbey
Carolingian hand first used in the 8th century

A Glastonbury Monk's prayer. (the Abbey and Black Designs)

The Manor House at Meare. (Penny Stokes) It was described by Abbot Beere's Surveyors as *large and beautiful*.

WEST MONKTON

It is possible that this manor was the subject of a grant to Abbott Hæmgils by King Centwine of 23 measures at *Cantucuudu* (Quantockwood?) in 682, and certainly Glastonbury held 15 measures at *Monechtone* in 1066.[104] A Beere terrier has not been traced but the *Valor* gives a figure of £59 14s. An imputed area of 2,438 acres at an average rent of 6.1d per acre has been entered. The estate, about three miles north-east of Taunton, was the abbey's most westerly possession, apart from Barslake in Monmouth. A P&M fragment notes '*60 acres now voyd in the Kyng's handes lately assigned to the prior of Taunton to fynd* (fund?) *a priest to say masses thrice a week in the almshouses'*. [105]

PODIMORE MILTON (Myddleton)

The Great Cartulary sees the origins of this property in an initial grant by King Edgar in 966. Further land was sold to the abbey by William de Myddleton in 1277; he was in debt both to the abbey and Jewish bankers and took this route to solvency. [106] The *Valor* put the estate at £23, and *circa* 1516 there were 784 acres of which 49% were arable. The average rent was 6.7d per acre and 22 tenants held an average of 36 acres each. Most tenants of this manor had a specific right to pasture oxen in 'Summerlease', at what appears to be a rent of 4d per ox per annum. P&M report no wood or waters within this lordship. They also report that '*the tenaunts of this manor are not a lyttle molested by oon Mr Light, for he of late hath stopped up a common waye which the said tenaunts tyme out of mynd have had over his ground to their ground which they now hold of the Kynges Majestie* (post Dissolution) *so that they cannot...take any proffit of their said ground as they have byne accustomed'*. [107] Clearly, disputes over rights of way are nothing new.

TABLE 5	Beere Total Acres	Beere Total Rent £	Rent d/acre	VE rent £	VE/ Beere diff. £s	Grass etc House & Bu'ld'ng acres	Arable Acres	Arable %	Common Acres*	Woods & Waters Acres*	No of Tenants	Av. Holding Acres*
GLASTONBURY TOWN												
Northlode by Glastonbury	747	32.5	10.4	31.3	-1.2	550	170	24%	0	27	23	31
Glaston' (incl c'mm'ns & moors)	7197	103.5	3.5									
& with imputed rents for i/h land	7197	225	10.0	328.9	0.9	3123	852	12%	2910	312	80	86
TOTALS	7944	361	10.9	360.2	-0.2	3574	1022	14%	2910	339	103	73
SOUTH SOMERSET												
Woods and commons as in the Pollard & Moyle surveys												
Broadwindsor	145	6.6	11.0	absent	0.0	6	123	95%	0	16	1	145
East Stoke	71	2.3	8.0	absent	0.0	34	37	52%	0		1	71
West Stoke	42	1.0	6.0	1.0	-0.1	Na	na	na	na	na	1	42
West Coker	100	2.5	6.0	3.0	0.5	na	na	na	na	na	3	33
Seavington	205	10.8	12.0	10.8	0.1	62	142.5	69%	0	0	7	29
TOTALS	563	23.2	9.9								13	43

GLASTONBURY TOWN and NORTHLODE (Table 5)

The origins of the core monastic holding around the town go back far beyond the Norman Conquest. One tradition (there are many) has it that St Philip dispatched 12 disciples to Britain in the first century AD. They were to *'introduce, in place of the barbarous and bloody rites long exercised by the bigotted and besotted druids, the meek and gentle system of christianity'*. The British King, Arivargus, was sufficiently impressed to allow them to settle around a small isle in Somerset with a hide of land each - the 'twelve hides of Glastonbury'. [108] However, it would seem that the original monks may have been granted an area much larger than that implied by twelve hides as currently understood. Within the range of 60-180 acres to a hide, the normally accepted spread, the original monks would only have had between 720 and 2,160 acres. However, the estate may well have been built up gradually by piecemeal gifts through the 7th and 8th centuries.

Just prior to the Dissolution, Glastonbury and Northlode alone comprised some 7,944 acres but to avoid delusions of accuracy, say 8,000 acres. Of this, some 2,250 acres would seem to have been kept in hand for the personal benefit of the abbot and convent. This land was not assigned a rental in Beere, which records £103 11s from tenant rents. An estimate of its rental value can however be made from a study of the land involved and its inclusion in the *Valor*. If the *Valor*'s commissioners applied an overall rental of 2s per acre to the 2,250 acres (i.e. £225), which they could well have done in view of the high quality of the property, there would have been a resultant valuation of £328, just £24 less than the *Valor* actually gives. The in-hand 2,250 acre demesne (or home farm), consisting of meadows, arable and parkland therefore had, it is suggested, an estimated annual value of some £225. A high figure but much fine-built property was

61

involved as well as the fertile parkland of Sharpham, Wirrall (now built over), Norwood and Pilton Park. Abbot Beere had built at Sharpham, as his own surveyors report, *'a fyne new house at his great expense, with chapel...storerooms and other handsome necessary domestic offices. With stone walls around...and sawn oak palings...apple orchards and fishpond and in which park it is possible to maintain 400 deer and 40 fat beasts each year and falconry in the hay meadows. The underwood here is not valued because it...is reserved for the use of the Lord Abbot'.* [109] A further description refers to this attractive property *'including orchards and long arbours...the parke contains 2 long myles in circuit of good meadow pasture with 2 fayre ponds, parke well paled and replenysshed with 160 deer of all sortes'.*

Abbot's Sharpham is still an imposing property and it was from here, on September 22nd 1539, that the aged Abbot Whiting was dragged away to his ultimate, vicious death. The role played in this by the King's Surveyors, Thomas Moyle and Richard Pollard along with Richard Layton, was unsavoury. [110] In writing to the Lord Privy Seal on September 23rd 1539 they say, *'We examined him* (the Abbot) *on certain articles and as his answers were not to our purpose, we advised him to call to his remembrance that which he had to then forgotten....'*

Wirrall Park, now absorbed into Glastonbury town, was recorded by P&M as having a *'gatehouse over the pale at the Keepers Lodge...lowe ground of wood and pasture plennysshed with 100 deer and a renning streme through the same'.* It also had the most valuable woodland if P&M reported accurately. (see page 18).

Arable land comprised only about 14% of the estate which, apart from the high quality 'home farm' of 2,250 acres, was dominated by the moors or levels (for all year grazing). Attaching to Glastonbury itself were some 3,200 acres of grazing moor, utilised in the main by the customary tenants. Allermore (1,040 acres) and Kennards Moor (430 acres) are shown on the current OS 1:50 000 map. With these common grazings included, the 103 tenants held an average of 73 acres each. There were five mills (two wind, two water and one horse-driven) yielding a total rent of £28 6s. In the *Valor* the annual value of hay taken from Sharpham, Wirrall and Pilton parks is shown at £5 10s.

Much of the income came from 80 or so town-houses and cottages in Glastonbury. These have been included in the overall income but excluded from estimates of agricultural rents and holding sizes. Included in the abbey estate was the building now known as the George and Pilgrim Hotel. A writer nearly 150 years after the Dissolution reported a secret passage from the abbey to the vaults of *'The George Inne with staires by which wee ascend to Abbots chamber very privately. In the chamber… is a faire An-cient Bedsteed wrought and guilded finely, here the Abbot, by the vault often came to this Inne and this chamber to Exercise himselfe Ad purgandos Renes (for the purging of his loins). The man of the House (Mr Dorvell) told mee that this bedsteed…is always reserved for the King (on his lease) for to use at his pleasure & in this room they say K.H.8 once lay.*[111]

MID SOMERSET and GLASTONBURY SUMMARY
The Mid Somerset properties together with Glastonbury and Northlode comprised the heart of the estate. Some 65,000 acres in all produced an income (or the potential) of £1,553 equivalent to 5.7d per acre.

SOUTH SOMERSET (Table 5)
Five small manors totalling about 550 acres have been located in South Somerset. Broadwindsor, with one demesne tenant on 123 acres paying 11d per acre; East and West Stoke and West Coker, in Beere but not clearly

identified in the *Valor*. The combined area of these four was probably about 350 acres. Beere records a dovecote at East Stoke where one tenant held 71 acres, of which 52% was arable, at 8d per acre. The fifth was seemingly Seavington St Michael, north-west of Crewkerne and known then as Sevenhampton Denys. The *Valor* and Beere valuations are almost the same at £10 16s and the best estimate of area is 205 acres, highly rented at 12d per acre. In 1482, the Crown took land in Dorset and gave Sevenhampton to Tewkesbury Abbey in exchange. However the land actually belonged to Glastonbury. After the conflicting grants were resolved, Glastonbury's ownership was confirmed in 1489. After the Dissolution, the manor passed to Winchester College, which only relinquished its interest in 1932. [112]

DORSET (Table 6)

No Beere terriers have been traced and only limited data has been found in P&M for the Dorset manors. The *Valor* has therefore been the main source of data and all acreages are imputed at the rental per acre shown in the table.

BUCKLAND NEWTON (Bukelonde)

The *Valor*'s figure is £73 2s. An acreage of 3,508 has been imputed. P&M listed 318 acres of common named as *Monke Wood hill, Doyle wood, Cosmore, Popling, Wykemarshe, Myllmarshe* and *Castell*. No woods were listed as such but the trees growing on these commons were valued in the great detail shown in all woodland surveys located. There were 1,735 individual trees with a total value of £80 - close to 1s per tree. The 15 *'grete okes'* were put at upwards of 5s each, *'lopped okes'* at 2s each and *'shrubbed okes'* 1s. *'Younge okes and asshes'* were put at 6d apiece. [113]

STURMINSTER NEWTON

The *Valor* figure is £93 12s with 5,616 acres being imputed at 4d per acre. A 2,000 acre common is noted in P&M [114] and is included in the foregoing figure. *'Diverse well set woods with great okes for tymber'*, are reported with an annual value of ten pounds, and P&M also note that, *'the scite of the howse standeth on a high hill just by a great ronning ryver in the valey... it is an ancyn buylding, portly and strong, able and mete for a knight to lye in...'*.
[115] P&M also note woods as: *Putellsworthe* 148 acres; *Pyle wood*, six acres with sufficient *'fyrebote'* and *'hedgbote'* reserved to the tenants with the pasture worth 12d per acre; *Lambes wood*, three acres with *'okes, elmes and asshes'*; *Fordes wood*, four acres, and *Fefys wood*, two acres in the tenancy of Robert Forde with the underlying pasture worth 4d per acre. Total woods amount to 238 acres including some common grazing.

TABLE 6

TABLE 6	Beere Total Acres	Beere Total Rent £	Rent d/acre	VE rent £	VE/ Beere diff. £s	Grass etc House & Build'ng acres	Arable Acres	Arable %	Common Acres*	Woods & Waters Acres*	No of Tenants*	Av. H'ld'ng Acres*
DORSET												
Buckland Newton (imputed)	3508		5.0	£73.10					318		110	
Sturminster Newton (imputed)	5616		4.0	£93.60					2000	268	140	
Marnhull (imputed)	2230		6.0	£55.75					80	100	70	
Byndon (imputed)	1066		6.0	£26.65							33	
TOTALS	12420		4.8	£249.10					2398	384	376	32
DEVON Uplyme	2490	£25.6	2.5	£25.90	0.3			not given	710	260	35	71
MONM'TH Bassaleg 5d/acre	1157	£24.1	5.0	£24.10							38	
TOTALS	3647	£50		£50.00	0.3						73	32*

*imputed at 32 acres per tenant

66

MARNHULL (Warnehall)

This has been imputed at 2,230 acres given a *Valor* figure of £55 15s. There were commons of 80 acres and '*divers woods*' totalling some 100 acres. A large freestone quarry was used mainly by the tenants for repairs but had an annual value of £2.[116]. There were fishings allocated '*in the river Stowey, every man after the rate of his ground abutting upon the Ryver aforesaid wherein he fisshes for sundry sortes as roche, pike, dace and trowte*'.

WYNFORD EAGLE (Byndon)

The *Valor* indicates that the Byndon property comprised the perpetual farm of Wynford (Wynford Eagle?) leased for £26 13s 4d per annum before the deduction of the fee of Christopher Lyatt, knight, the bailiff there. Byndon has been imputed to contain 1,066 acres at 6d per acre.

DORSET SUMMARY

Using average rents determined in relation to the agricultural nature of the estates and the rentals shown in the *Valor*, it is estimated that Glastonbury held about 12,750 acres in Dorset at the Dissolution.

DEVON (Table 6)

UPLYME

This estate, dating from the mid-10th century as a Glastonbury possession, [117] is fully documented in both Beere and P&M. It comprised some 2,490 acres *circa* 1516, stretching up from the sea at Ware in a sausage shape to Furzeleigh Farm, north of Raymond Hill. P&M (as reassessed by McGregor) give 2,434 acres; in both surveys there were some 710 acres of common grazing on the downland at Wolcombe Downe and Rolcombeshed and the 260 acre Wolcombe Wood.[118]. These extensive areas reduced average rents to less than 3d per acre. Excluding these commons, rents averaged 5d. The 68% grass demesne was let to Thomas Swayne for an average 8d per acre. Beere records that Robert Rycheman held a messuage called 'Kytthouse', a garden, orchard, six acres of meadow and the water mill rented for 8s per annum with the tenants required to assist him with maintenance of the millpond and the pinfold.

P&M record certain tenancy terms: *'The tenaunts of this manor take their Ten[ancy] for term of a life or lives as many as they can agree with the lord. And the wife of every tenaunt dieing she, not being named in the copie, during her widow[hood] shall have and enyoie the term which her husband had'*. [119] The latter provision seemed universal on Glastonbury estates judging by the frequency with which 'widow' appears after a female name in the lists of customary tenants.

MONMOUTH (Table 6)

BARSLAKE. (Bassaleg in Wallia).
Bassaleg was granted to Glastonbury by Robert de la Hay in the early 12th century. [120] Both Beere and the *Valor* figure for the property, which lies immediately to the west of Newport, was £24 2s before deduction of the 6s 8d fee of the bailiff, John Hoptkyns. A rent of 5d per acre has been imputed to give an area of 1,157 acres.

Appendix A   Perambulation of Street

Set out below is the preamble to and the details of Abbot Beere's perambulation of the boundaries of Street, which, in common with all of the Beere terriers, prefaces the listing of tenants.

Strete

Lands All the lands and tenements with the fines rents and heriots of this manor made here in the month of March in the seventh year of King Henry 8's reign and the twenty-second year of the Lord Abbot Richard Beere before brother Thomas Sutton the *forinsec* cellarer on the oath and fealty of Thomas Boddon, bailiff and the reeve here John Baker, Thomas Gyet, Thomas Seywell, Robert Rode, William Walter and all other tenants of the lord here for the said lands here separately and distinctly perambulated, measured and approved/sworn to.

Boundaries of the manor. There exist here the following bounds and boundary stones [recorded by] Brother Thomas Sutton, *forinsec* cellarer of the monastery of Glastonbury, William Lang, clerk/auditor of the aforesaid monastery, Thomas Gunwyn, Thomas Somerset clerks of the said monastery, Thomas Boddon, bailiff of the manor and the above tenant jurors and also all the other tenants of the said manor and those of the adjoining township. Beginning to the south-east of the demesne farm here at *Brutesaysshe* now called *Three Aysshes* growing in the south-east area of Street bridge and from there directly eastward as far as *Bythehurne* and thence east to *Attelake* south whence next to *Blackgrove* and thence south-east as far as *Growethamesoke* and from there south-east as far as *Wottonsdore alias Wottonsdrove* and thence south-westerly by the dyke called *Growthamesdych* as far as Growthames? *ford* and thence south upstream as far as the watercourse goes to *Butterpyll* in the south part of *Whethullam* and thence south-west along the aforesaid stream as far as *Wottonford* and thence south-west by the stream as far as the boundary stone at the wood of *Longhegge alias lez Holthegge* and thence south by the said hedge to the boundary stone at *Worthyhyll* and then westward for some 8 perches to the wood in the area of the said *langhegge* and then south by the hedge to the boundary stone at *Lyholtcorner* and then west for 10 perches to a boundary stone and then ascend southwards towards the hill between the lordship of *Buddecly* (Butleigh) and Strete to the King's Road between *Kyneweston* and *Pouldon* and then west by the said road to the cross standing next to *Strowterselins* that stands in the middle of the road here. Then west by the ridge to a boundary stone situated in the southern area of the quarry viz between the land of the Abbot of Glastonbury and that of John Marshall of *Ivethorn* then the ploughland as far as the higher part of *Cleyfurlong* then west by the said road to the *Landshere* (boundary bank) between the lordships of Strete and Walton and then north by the bank to the northern side of *Holwelswale* and then east for 5 perches to *Chalkwelsbroke* and then north by the stream to the southern part of *Challwellynch* and then north to *Challwell* and so to the ford between Walton and Strete and then north-west as the stream descends to the boundary of *Avesneyclose* and this is beyond the bound. Then to the south and west angle of the close called *Palinsclose* which is beyond the bound and then east to *Ffeyrethorne* which is beyond and then south to the wood in the eastern corner of *Howndwode* and then east to the north-east corner of *Lordyclyz* and so east by the middle close called *Grenes Close* to *Brutesaysshe* at the *Aysshes* bound where it began.

Appendix B Customary Tenancy - Record of an individual holding at Baltonsborough.

Set out below is the full detail of an individual holding at Baltonsborough. All entries in the Beere terriers followed a generally similar pattern, probably due to the guiding hand of Brother Thomas Sutton and this record of **Henry Kyngdon's holding** may be taken as reasonably typical of the 2,000 or so entries examined.

'Fine' £20

Henry Kyngdon, half-virgate tenant, holds one messuage with curtilage, garden and orchard containing one acre.

Likewise, he holds 35½ acres and half a rood of meadow and pasture in severalty wherein, annexed to the aforesaid curtilage, in seven fields are 16 acres. In *Buttmore* (demesne) 4 acres. In *Park Close* 7½ acres and ½ rood. In *Chalcrofte* 8 acres (demesne). Likewise he holds one grove of oke and ash called *La Parke* containing 4 acres.

Likewise, he holds 2 acres of meadow in the common meadow called *Honeymede* wherein next to *Kyngton* is mede' one acre and in Orfurlong one acre.

Likewise he holds 24¾ acres of arable land in two fields wherein in the north field at *Lugbourne* 3 acres; at *Colaswell* one acre called *Hedacre*; at *Gateway* ½ acres; at *Colaswell* 1½ acres in two plots; in eastern part of *Foteland* 8 acres in 2 plots; at *Hethstones furlong* 2 acres. And in the south field above *Langdowne* 2 acres. In *Yoo furlong* 3¾ acres in 4 plots; at *Cattyshameline* ½ acre; in *Orchardhyll furlong* 2½ acres in 2 plots.

Rent 46 shillings.

And when he dies he gives a heriot.

The above data was summarised as follows: total land 69 acres (grass 40, arable 25, wood 4); rent 46s; average rent per acre, 8d.

Note: Fines or more accurately, entry premiums were levied on a succession but no link could be found between the amount of premium shown and the size of the holding. The quality of the house and buildings may have been a relevant factor not easy to determine after nearly 500 years. The amount paid and the term of years or lives may well have been negotiated and subject to market forces. (This principle seems to apply in the Uplyme terrier, (see page 68). A heriot was a death duty payable to the landlord, usually the best beast on the holding. By the Dissolution, this may usually have been commuted to a cash payment especially as the monks would only have to sell the beast to perhaps unwilling local buyers. It would be tough on a newly widowed woman to lose not only her husband but her most valuable animal as well.

Appendix C. Glastonbury Bailiffs in 1536

Name	Manor	Annual Fee
	As named and shown in the *Valor*	
William Walton	Aisshecote	24s
Thomas Pressey	Aissheby (Berks)	26s 8d
William Morce	Badbury	13s 4d
William Cock	Baltonsborough	33s 4d
John Hoptkyns	Barselake in Wallia	6s 8d
Robert Coward	Batcombe	26s 8d
William Borough	Berghes	23s 4d
Sir Chris. Lyatt	Byndon	20s
Richard Parker	Bradleigh	10s
John Porter	Buckelond (Dorset)	54s 8d
Walter Adamps	Butleigh	20s 8d
Robert Hyatt	Chrismalford	26s 8d
John Hilliard	Dychesiaett	26s 8d
Edward Somerset	Domerham	46s 8d
John Colefer	Doultyng	22s 8d
Robert Dover	Estebrent	43s 4d
William Vowles	Estpennard	26s 8d
Thomas Fuller	Estrete (Glaston')	3s 4d
Thos Bull, Thos Pester, Nicholas Aisher & John Gould	Glastonbury	£8
No bailiff (land let by indenture)	Goderihay	
Robert Heitt	Greyngton	16s 10d
Edward Bristowe	Grutlyngton	20s
John Paddock	Hamme	25s
Robert Worth	Idmyston	26s
Richard Snell	Kyngton	28s
John Bowser (steward)	Dev' ll Langbrigge	20s
William Bryce (bailiff)	(Longbridge Deverill)	13s 4d
Robert Docker	Lympelsham	20s
Thomas Clowde Hundestert &	Merkysbury	16s 8d
Thomas Row	Marnehull	33s 4d
Richard Lyne	Mere	26s 8d
John Horner	Mellez	25s
Henry Cary	Middelsowye	£1 6s 8d

John Bord	Myddelton	£1s 3s 4d
William Bryce Este	Monketon	10s
Paul Crasse	Netylton	20s
Thomas Row (Sturminister)	Newton	33s 4d
William Brownyng	Northlode (Glaston')	26s 8d
William Mylward,	Otherey	£1 6s 8d
Richard Broderybbe &	Pedwell, Shapwyck	
John Frye	Sutton Sowey	
	& Murelynch	61s 4d
John Broderybbe	Pilton	33s 4d
Thomas Baker	Sevynhampton Denys	10s
William Walton	Shapwyck	31s 8d
William Bowdon	South Brent	20s
Robert Compton	Strete	25s 6d
John Rede	Uplyme (Devon)	13s 4d
John Dagon	Walton	26s 8d
John Shattock	West Monkton	26s 8d
Thomas Whyting &		
Richard Broderybbe	Westpennard	60s
John Protte	Weston (Zoyland)	£1 6s 8d
Nicholas Sloper	Wynterbourne	
	(Monkton)	13s 4d
John Weston	Wythis	7s
William Lang &		
John Beks	Wryngton	57s 8d

Appendix D.   Names of Tenants.

There follows a full alphabetical listing of all the individual tenants/occupiers named for the estates for which Abbot Beere's terriers have been located. (w) denotes widow; (d) demesne farmer; (B) bailiff; Kt Knight; free, freeman.

74

Occupier

John Abbellyes
Helena Abbott
John Abbot
John Abyn
John Acombe
William Aconb
Thos Acourt
Nicholas Adam
Robert Adam
Stephen Adam
Richard Adam
William Adam
John Adam
Andreas Adame
Wm Adames
John Adamps
Wm Adamps
John Adamps
John Adams jnr
Joanna Adams (w)
Helena Adams (w)
Wm Adams
John Adams
Alice Adams
Christin' Adams (w)
Thos Adams
John Adelot (free)
R. Adnipe
Richard Aldey
John Aleyn
William Aleyn
George Alford
Henry Alford
Wm Algar
John Algar
Marjorie Allfield
Edward Allond
Wm Allwyn
Wm Alne
John Alne
John Alwyn
Simon Alwyn
John Alyn
Elena Alyn
William Ambuler
John Ambuler
Wm Amore

Robert Amort
John Amos Jnr
John Amos
Walter Amyett
John Androwes
Robt. Anney
Thos Anyett
John Anyne
John Aphoell (taylor)
Thos Aphowell
John Asshe
John Atmapull
John Attaey
John Attavasse
John Atteford
Thomas Atteford
John Atteford
Richard Attewell
William Attewey
John Attewey
Henry Attewey
M'rgry Attewode (w)
John Attewode
John Attewode
Robert Attewood
John Attewull
John Attewull snr
John Atteyee
Agnes Atteyoo
William Atteyou
Bernard Aysheley
Richard Ayssh
John Ayssham
Thos Aysshe
John Aysshly

Alice Babbe (w)
Robert Backage
Thomas Bailly
Richard Bailly
John Bailly
Wm Bakehouse
John Baker snr
Jon Baker
Wm Baker
Thomas Baker (B)
John Baker

Joanna Baker (w)
Richard Baker
John Baker jnr
Henry Baker
John Baker jnr
Henry Baker
Thos Baker
Isabella Balard (w)
William Balche (d)
William Ballett
Thos Ballett
Stephen Bampton
John Bampton
Walter Banwell
Isabella Bardon (w)
John Barghe
Wm Barghe
Wm Atte Barghe
John Barley
John Barlo
Walter Barnard
John Barne
Richard Barom
Robert Baron
John Baron
John A Barough
Thos Barrdyn
John Barrell
Robert Bartelatt
Christ'pher Bartlett
Rich'rd Baryington
William Basse
Juliana Batcock (w)
Wm Batcock
Robert Batyn
John Batyn snr
John Batyn jn
Walter Baugh
Wm Bawdon
Robert Bawdon
Wm Bawdon snr
Wm Bawdon jnr
Richard Bawe
John Bawe
Thos Bayley
John Baylly
John Baylye

John Beamonde
Wm Beer
Joanna Beer (w)
Wm Beere
Walter Beffyld
John Beke
Henry Bell
Robert Bell
John Bember
Wm Benatt
Thomas Bennett
John Bennett snr
Wm Bennett
John Benott
John Benyng
Wm Beoley
Thos Berghe jnr
John Beryle
Thomas Beryll (free)
John Besseley
Wm Bevtll
Walter Bevyle
William Bevyle
Thomas Bevyle
Wm Bilhey
Henry Bine
Agnes Black (w)
John Blackewode
    (baker)
Wm Blackmarn
Wm Blake
John Blysse
Helen Bocher
John Bocher
Robert Bodden
Thos Boddon
Robert Bodyn
John Bolloffer
William Bonde
Katrina Borde
John Borde (d)
John Borgh
Thos Borgh snr
R'b'rt Boucher (free)
Wm Bouer
John Bourton jnr
John Bourton snr

Occupier

Robert Bourton
Simon Bourton
Robert Boveton
Wm Bower
John Bowton
Isabel Boxe
Margaret Boyce
John Boyton
John Branche
Wm Braye
John Brent (free)
Richard Bretayne
John Brewer
Edward Bristowe (B)
Steph'n Broderybbe
John Broderybbe
Rich'rd Broderybbe
Richard Brodeylbe
John Broke (free)
John Broke
John Brokewyn
Richard Brokewyn
Richard Bronn
John Bronn
William Brown
Walter Brown
Nicholas Browne
Marg'ret Browne (w)
Wm Browne
Thos Browning
Wm Browning (d)
Wm Browning
Thos Browning
William Browning
William Brownyng (B)
John Brownyng
John Brownyng
John Brugge
Thos Atte Brugge
Thos Brugge
Laurence Brugge
John Brugge snr
William Bryce
Joanna Bryce (w)
John Bryce
John Bryce jnr
Robert Bryce

John Brygge Jnr
Richard Brygge
John Brympton
Thos Brytayne
Wm Bucke
John Budde
Wm Buddebrigge
Thos Bulcing
John Bulgeon
Thos Bulgeon
John Bulgion
Alice Bulgion
John Bulke
Stephen Bullock
Laurence Bullock
John Bullock
William Bullock
William Bulte
John Bulte
John Bulting
Thos Bultyng
Wm Bunse
John Burdenhame
John Burdham
John Burgeeys
Walter Burgens
Thos Burgers
Nicholas Burges
Philip Burges
Richard Burgeys
John Burgeys
Agnes Burgeys
John Burr
Richard Buryatt
Alicia Buryett (w)
William Buryman
Richard Buryman
Thos Buryman
Richard Busshe
Robert Busshe
Henry Buysshe
Agnes Byde
John Bykemer
Thos Byndoe
WmByndoe
Laurence Byndoe
George Byngley

Wm Bysseley
Robert Bysshopp
Thos Bysshopp
John Bysshopp
Thos Bysshopp
John Bythesee
Walter Bythesee
John Bythesee jnr
Henry Bythsee
Rbt. Bythsee
    (water bailiff)

Edigius Cabbell
John Cabbull
Margaret Cabell
John Calon
John Calowe
John Capon
John Capron
Walter Carey (d)
Valentius Carpenter
William Carter
Richard Carter
Wm Cary
Alice Cary (w)
Thomas Cary
Richard Cary
Walter Castell
Humphrey Causer
Robert Cayles
John Celerar
John Chaloner
John Challener
Wm Champion
John Champion
Richard Champion
John Champyon
John Champyon jnr
Robert Champyon
Wm Champyon
John Chapel
Ed. Chapell
John Chapell
Edward Chapell
John Chapman
Edith Chapman
Richard Chaton

John Chaton
Walter Chaton
William Chaton
Richard Chatone
John Chelcrofte
John Chelcrofte snr
Richard Child
Robert Child
Wm Child
Thos Chowne
Thos Churchouse
Churchwardens
Agnes Chyke (w)
Wm Chyke
John Chyn
Margey Chynne (w)
John Chynne
John Clappe
John Clapper
Phil.Clarke
Nicholas Clement
Edward Clement
    (soldier)
John Clemment snr
John Clement jnr
Wm Clerk
Thom Clerk
Thos Clerke
Wm Clerke jnr
Wm Clerke
Robt. Clerke
John Clerke Snr
Thos Clerks
John Clerks jnr
Thos Cleve
Thom Cleve
Peter Cock
John Cocke
Alice Cocke (w)
Rbt. Cocke
Wm Cocke (B)
Thos Cocke
Robert Cockes
Helena Cocks
Richard Cockys
John Cockys
Wm Coe

Occupier

John Cogan
Thos Coke
John Coke
Robert Coke
Richard Coke
William Coke
Nicholas Coke
R'b'rt Colchester
Simon Cole
Richard Cole
Robert Coleman
Richard Coliford
John Collerigge
John Collock
John Collys
Wm Collys
Robert Collys
Walter Collys
Robert Colman
Dionisius Colman
John Colyar
John Colyer jnr
John Colyer
John Colyford
John Colyns
Robert Colyns
Wm Combe snr
Thos Combe jnr
John Combe
Wm Combe jnr
Thos Combe
Edmund Come
Edm'nd Comeldon
Thos Compton
John Condeland
Richard Constabul
John Cooke
Richard Cooke
John Cope
Wm Cope
Thos Coperer
William Coppe
Tholom'n Coppe
Thol Coppe
John Cornishe
John Cornyce
John Cornysshe

Robert Cory
William Corye
John Coryngdon
William Cosyn
ThosCotehyll
John Cotgyll
John Cottyn snr
Robert Councell
Richard Counsell
Edith Courte (w)
Wm Courteney Kt
R'ch'rd Cowbor'we
Wm Cowly
Wm Cowlyn
Robert Cox
Roger Craddock
Thos Crane
Richard Crandon
Paul Crasse (B)
Wm Credenhull
Richard Crese
John Crese snr
Robert Crese
John Crese jnr
William Cretayn
Robert Crey
Richard Crosby
John Crose
John Crosseman
Thos Crosseman
Thos Crossways
Robert Crowson
John Cryche
Philip Cryvett
Thos Culberry
John Curteys
John Cutler
Hugh Cutteler
John Cutteler
John Cuttell
John Cutton

John Dagon (B)
John Dalar
Richard Dale
John Dane
John Davy

William Davy
Thos Davy
John Daye
Katrina Dayle
John Deen
Nicholas Deen
Thomas Deer
Wm Deere
Richard Deigh
Wm Deigh
Demesne harvester
Joanna Deneawde
John Denys
William Dernell
 Nicholas De'tell (d)
John Devall
John Deverill
Wm Dewadon
John Dey
WmDey
Wm Deye
John Deye
John Deygh
William Deyman
Lawrence Dobell
Richard Dober
Thos Dobyn
Wm Dogoode
Richard Doker
Richard Done
John Donman
John Donne
Wm Donnyate
Ld Donvelede
Wm Door
Dr Wm Dorsatt
John Dorsatt
John Dove
John Dowdyng
John Drake
John Draper
Christina Drew
John Dudde
Nicholas Duke
John Dulting
Richard Dun
John Dun

William Dun
Thos Dun
John Dunkerton Snr
John Dunkerton
Wm Dunkerton
Richard Dunn
John Dunn
Thomas Dyer
John Dyett
Wm Dyke
John Dynghurst
Richard Dyutt
John Dyutt jnr
Robert Dyutt
John Dyverice (d)

Thomas Edward
Agnes Edward
Wm Edward
John Edwarde
Thomas Edwards
Walter Egie
Richard Ellen
Edith Ellen
Wm Elme
John Elyott
Walter Elys
Nicholas Emlyn
Hugo Eston
Wm Eston
Walter Eynon
John Eynon

Thos Farre
John Feirby
Mary Felde
John Feldhouse
John Fenne
Wm Fetreby jnr
John Fetyplace
Thos Feyreby
Richard Feyreby
Wm Feyreby
John Ffeers
John Fferton
Richard Fford
John Ffox

77

Occupier

Edward Ffoxe
Henry Ffoxe
Wm Ffoxe
Nicholas Ffrenshe
Thos Ffrey
Marguerita Ffrye
Richard Ffynner
John Ffynner
John Fitzjames Kt
Thos Fitzpaine
Thos Fitzpayne
Wm Fitzpayne
Lucy Flather
Joana Flyvyan
John Foliet
John Fonteyn
John Forde
Thomas Forde
Wm Forde
Thos Forest
John Forty
Robert Fortune
Wm Fox
John Fox
John Freeman
John Frenshe
B'rth'lm'w Frenshe
Thos Frenshman
John Fry
Richard Fry
John Fry
John Frye sn
John Frye jn
WmFrye
Thos Fussell
John Fychatt
Robt. Fychett
John Fysshe
Thos Fyssher
William Fyssher
Wm Fyssher

Richard Gache
Simon Gage
Cecilye Gage
Wm Gage
Alice Game (w)

Thos Gammyche
Alice Gammyche
Thos Gamyge
John Gamyge
John Gangell jnr
Thos Gangell
Agnes Gangell (w)
Robert Gangell
Robert Garden
Robert Gardener
William Gardiner
Agnes Gardner (w)
John Garrett
John Garrett jnr
Robert Gaterygge
John Gaylard
Alice Genett (w)
John Gennet
Simon Gentyll
John German
John Gerves
John Gerveys
Agnes Gibelett (w)
Agnes Gleys
William Glympton
John Gode
William Godefrey
John Godehyn
Edith Goderd
William Godeson
Nicholas Godfrey
Richard Godfrey
Thos Godfrey
Rbt Godwyn
John Godwyn
John Godyn
Thos Godynch
John Golde
Wm Golde
Sibella Goldsmith
Robert Goodelle
John Goodelle
Stephen Goodeson
Ag. Gorle
Joanna Gorney
Wm Gould
John Gould

Robert Goulde
Wm Gounchie
John Gounchie
Wm Goundenham
Thos Gradock
John Gramond
Thos Gray
Richard Green
John Gregory
Richard Grene
Thos Grenwyn
Wm Greve
Stephen Grey
Wm Grey
John Grey
Robert Grey
John Griffyth
Richard Grigge
Richard Grose
Juliana Grove (w)
John Groves
Philip Growe
Thomas Growe
Richard Growe
Wm Growe
Juliane Growe (w)
John Growe
William Growe
John Gryce
Robert Gryce snr
Robert Gryce jnr
Richard Grygge
Thos Gunwyn (d)
Philip Gunwyn
Walter Gust
John Guste jnr
John Guste snr
Katerina Gyan
John Gyan
John Gyatt
Richard Gyatt
John Gybbs (d)
Robert Gye
Wm Gyell
Radulphus Gyfford
John Gyle
Thomas Gyle

William Gyle
Agnes Gyle (w)
John Gyles
Peter Gyles
John Gylle
Thos Gylle
Nicholas Gylling
Thomas Gylling
John Gylling
Richard Gylling
Agnes Gyllyng
Richard Gyllyng
John Gyllyng
William Gylmyn
John Gyott
Thos Gyotte (d)
Richard Gyre
Walter Gyste

Alice Haberfeld (w)
Richard Haberfield
Joanna Hacche
Richard Hacche
John Hache
William Hacke
John Halle
Wm Halle
John Halsey
Thos Hambrigge
La Hame
John Hamlyn
John Hancock
Thomas Hannam
John Hardewyll
Richard Harding
Wm Hardwell
Simon Hardwell
William Hardying
John Hardyng jn
John Hardyng sn
John Hares
Richard Hares
Wm Hares
Stephen Harmon
Sibilla Harold (w)
Wm Harres
Thomas Harries

Occupier

John Harries
Wm Harries
Richard Harries
Edith Harries (w)
Henry Harries
John Harryes
Wm Harryes
Wm Harveys
John Haryes
Hugo Haryes
Wm Hasley Snr
John Hatherell
John Hatherwell
Radolphus Hatt
Henry Haukyns
Robert Haverance
John Hawell
Richard Hawkins
Thos Hawkins
Wm Hawkyns Jnr
Wm Hawkyns
Richard Haydon
Henry Hayles
John Hayne
Thomas Hayne
John Hayne
Rbt. Hayne snr
Peter Hayward
John Hayward
John Hebbeston
Wm Helyatt
Wm Hemery
John Herbord Snr
John Herford
Sible Herse
Wm Herte
Richard Hether
John Hewse
John Hewys
Wm Hicke
Wm Hickyngr
Wm Hilbert
Sybil Hill (w)
John Hining
Wm Hipper
Wm Hipysleyghe
John Hirneman

John Hobbes jnr
John Hobbes snr
Thomas Hobbs
John Hobbs
George Hobby
William Hobbys
John Hobbys
Robert Hobbys
John Hobbys
Richard Hodde
William Hogge
John Hogges
John Hogges
Robert Hoggs
Alicia Hoggs (w)
William Hoggs
Thos Hoggs
John Hokulbrigge
John Holder snr
John Holder jnr
Stephen Hole
John Hole
John Hollewaye
John Holman
John Honchyns
John Honchyns
John Honycot
John Hooper
Agnes Hooper (w)
John Hop
Richard Hoper
Richard Hopkyns
Robert Horne
John Horner (B)
Thos Horner
Richard Horte
Robert Horton snr
Edward Horton
Thos Horton
Robert Horton jnr
Wm Hortte
John Horyce (free)
Robert Hotchines
John House
John Howell
John Howleigh
John Hukulbrugge

Wm Hukulbrugge
John Hunt
Henry Hunt
Walter Hunt
Robert Hunte
Richard Huntlely
Richard Hurde
John Hurmen
Thos Hurneman
John Hurvema
Wm Hutchyns
Wm Hutchyns jnr
William Hyatte
Joanna Hyatte (w)
John Hycke
Wm Hydon
Nicholas Hylle
Robt. Hyllard
WmHyll
John Hyll
John Hyll jnr
Edward Hyll
Hugo Hyll
Wm Hyll
Robert Hylpe
Wm Hyppyn

John Isgar

John Jackelott
Thos Jacob
Sussanna Jacob
John Jakeman
John Jamys
Thos Janes
Thos Janes
Nicholas Janett
John Janyns
John Janyns snr
Wm Jay
Thos Jefferies
John Jeffryes
Richard Jenkins
Wiliam Jesopp
John Jesopp
Robert Joce
Thos Joce

Walter Jocelyn
Edward Jones
Wm Jones
Thos Jones
Robert Joyce
Peter Jurmyn
Henry Jurmyn

Thomas Kayser
John Kayser
Robert Kayser
John Kempe
Robert Kendal
John Kene
Wm Kenning
John Keorle
Robert Keorle
William Keorle
Robert Kew
Thomas Keytengall
John Kindeman jnr
John Kindeman
Wm Kindeman
Thos Kineman jnr
Walter Kingman
Richard Kirby
William Knappe
John Knappe
Thos Knappeloke
John Kychewyn
John Kylbury
Walter Kyndeman
Richard Kyng
Wm Kyng
Henry Kyngdon
Wm Kyngesbury
John Kyngton
Robert Kyngysbry
John Kynman

Thos Lacey
Alice Lacey
John Lachame
John Lacy
Joanna Lamb
Wm Lane
John Lane

Occupier

Alex Laneman
Wm Lang (B)
Henry Lang Esq
  (fishings)
Robert Lang
Richard Lang jnr
John Lange
John Larcamb
John Larcomb
John Lardar Kt
John Laueraunce
Wm Laurance
Thos Laurence
Walter Lavenham
John Lavenham
Robt. Lavenhome
Robert Laverance
William Laverius
John Laverquince
John Lawetre
John Lawtree
Nicholas Lay
Wm Lecky
Wm Lemman
John Lenge
Thomas Lenge
Thos Leoky
John Leoky
Wm Leoky
John Leoky
Thos Leonge
Wm Leonge
Edith Leste
William Leste
Edm'nd Leveregge
David Lewys
Thos Leyghton Kt
John Lighe
Thos Lock
Philip Lock
Richard Locke
Robert Locke
John Locke
John Lodryn
Thos Lodryn
William Lodryn
Robert Lodwyll

John Lodwyn
William Lodwyn
Agnes Loker
Cecelia Lomehouse
John London
Richard Long
Thos Lovecock
John Lovecock
John Lovekye
Thos Lovell
John Lovell
Robert Lovibond
John Lovybond
Wm Lovybond
W'm Lovybound
Thos Lovybound
John Luckyng
John Luifyn
Robert Lurifin
Wm Luyde
Wm Lyde
Thos Lydyard
Philip Lyllyng
John Lynde
John Lyneng
John Lyon Jnr

Marg'r't Mann (w)
Robert Mann
John Manne
John Manstiche
John atte Mapull
John Marey
Richard Mareys
Wm Maron
Wiliam Marrys
John Marshal Kt
Walter Martyn
Thomas Martyn
John Martyn
Henry Martin
William Maryes
William Maryne
John Maryne
John Maryner
John Maryner
Thom Maryner

John Maryner
Thos Maryner
Wm Marys jnr
Wm Marysshe jnr
Wm Marysshe snr
William Mason
John Mason
Thomas Master
William Masy
Richard Mayne
Richard Maynard
Joanna Maynstone
Robert Mayoo
John Mayoo
Thomas Mayoo
Medarius of Glaston
Wm Merchant
William Mere
Richard Mere
Ralph Mericke
Richard Merke (free)
Wm Merlowe
John Merner
Richard Mersshe
John Mey jnr
John Mey
John Mey
Thomas Michael
Richard Michell
John Michell
John Miller
John Millward
John Mockesegge
John Mogge
Thos Moke
Thos Moke jnr
Thomas Molenxe
Isabella Moleyns(w)
Philip Moleyns
John Molyns
Richard Moore
Thos Morar
John Morcock
John Mordey
Thos More
William More
  (blacksmith)

Richard More
Thos More
John More (d)
Wm More
Robert More
John Morecock
Wm Morefyld
John Morgan
Joanna Morris
Thos Mors
Richard Mors
John Mors
Wm Morse
John Morse
Richard Morys
Thomas Morys
Lord Mounfort
Alice Mower (w)
John Mulward
John Mulward jn
John Mulward sn
John Mustard
R'bert Mydwynter
William Myghell
Wm Mylebourne
Agnes Mylkyn (w)
Thos Mylkyn
Thos Mylle
John Mylle
Robert Mylle
John Mylward
George Mytton

Wm Nayshe
Wm Necke
Robert Nellen
John Neott
Wm Nevyle
Alice Neweman
Thos Newman
Joanna Neyll
Wm Nicholl
John Nicoll
John Nicolls
Richard Nicotte
Robert Nobyll
Thos Norington

Occupier

Clement North (d)
John Northern
John Northeyn
John Northfolk
Ric' Notebromius
John Notebromius
Margaret Noyle (w)
Edmund Nycolas
John Nycoll
John Nycolls
Agnes Nycotte (w)
William Nycotte
John Nywe
John Nyweman
Nicholas Nyweton

Robert Oakley
Johanna Odam.(w)
Willam Odamps
Marg'ry Odamps(w)
Richard Odyan
Alicia Offer
Thos Offer
John Offer
Thomas Ogan
Joanna of Oke (w)
William of Oke
John of Oke snr
Henry of Oke
John of Oke jnr
John Osmond
John Osmonde
Richard Othery
Robt. Othery

Nicholas Pady
Robert Pagan
John Page
Robert Page
Wm Page
William Paige
John Pallewebbe
John Palmer
Thomas Palmer
John Parely
Walter Parelyn
John Parker

Thomas Parker
Robert Parker
Edith Parker (w)
Thos Parker jnr
Henry Parsin
John Parson
Robert Parson
Thomas Parson
Henry Parson
John Parson jnr
John Parys
Thomas Pathe
John Pathlocke
John Pathlocks
J'hn Pathlocks jn
John Paty (free)
Robert Paul
William Paveley
Wm Payne
John Payne (d)
Richard Payne
Henry Paynott
Richard Paynter
John Pearson
Richard Peers
John Peers
Thos Peers
John Pennard
John Peny
Wm Peorle
John Pereham (d)
John Perhine
Richard Perkys
John Perry
William Persan
John Pesto
John Pety
William Pety
John Peverell
Thos Pewe
Alice Pheleps
John Phelpes
William Phelpes
John Phelpys (free)
John Philypps
Thos Phippayn
Henry Pleasans

John Plenty
Philippa Plenty (w)
William Plummer
Simon Pody
Thomas Pollard
Henry Pope
Thos Pope
John Pope
Edith Popyll (w)
Humphrey Popyll
John Porch
John Porche
Selwyn Pore
Edw'rd Porkeswell
Richard Porter
Joanna Porter (w)
John Portor
John Potter jn
John Potter
Richard Potter
Thomas Pounsatt
Richard Powes
Amyas Powlett Kt
John Powlett (free)
Thos Prat
Walter Pratman
Margaret Press
William Pride
John Pride
Henry Pride
Thomas Pronte
Rev.Thos Prowte
John Pryde
Richard Pryde
Thom Pryde jnr
Thos Pryde
William Pryde
Thos Prynce
Thos Pulver
Jo.Punyman
   (painter)
John Purcheys
John Purde
John Pury
Robert Puryton
John Pyke
Wm Pypett

John Pytt
Richard Pytte
John Pytte snr
Thos Pytte
John Pytte jnr
Agnes Pytteney

John Quarriman
Walter Quick

John Rafe
John Ramesbury
Isabella Rawlyns (w)
Richard Raynod
John Raynold
John Raynsbury
Thos Rayser
Wm Rechyn
John Rede (d)
William Rede
John Rede (B)
Thomas Rede
Isabella Rendell (w)
Thos Reode
John Riche
Roger Riche
John Rixe Jnr
John Robarts
John Robyns
Thos Robyns
Wm Robyns
John Robys
John Roc
John Rode
John Rode (attorney)
John Rode at Cross
Robert Rode
Robert Rode
Stephen Rode
Robert Rode
Wm Rogers
John Rogers
Alice Rogers (w)
Wm Roleigh
John Roley
Wm Roley
John Roligh

Occupier

John Roligh(taylor)
John Roly
William Roly
John Roo
John Roode
Wm Rooley
John Rooley
Margaret Rosay
Peter Roweland
John Rowett
Wm Royle
John Royle
Thos Rusdene
John Rush
Walter Rushe
Isabell Russell (w)
Robert Russell
Joanna Russhe (w)
Thos Rustie
Thos Rycardes
John Rychards
Richard Ryche
Nicholas Ryche
Richard Rycheman
William Rycheman
Marg'r't Rycheman
Wm Rymell
Walter Rymell
Thos Rywe
Thomas Ryx
John Ryx snr
Richard Ryxe

Augustus Sadler
William Salay jnr
John Salisbury
John Sammell snr
Thos Sampson
Robert Samuel
Wm Samuel
Wm Sanber
John Sangell
John Saunders
Robert Saunders
George Sawyer
Wm Say
John Sayard

John Sayarde
John Saye
Robert Saye
Robert Saye
John Saye
Wm Scoton
Robert Scott
John Scotte
Robert Scotte
John Scotton
John Scottyn jnr
Wm Scottyn
John Scottyn snr
John Scotyn
William Scoytte
John Seargeant
Juliana Segard (w)
John Sellesson
William Sellisson
Wm Selman
John Selson
Walter Sely
Roger Sergent
William Servington
Wm Servyes
Walt.Sevington (free)
Wm Sevyar
Thos Sevyer
John Sevyer
Wm Seward
John Seward
Thom. Sewell
Thom Sewell
John Sewell (free)
John Shearwood
John Sheotar snr
Wm Sheotar
John Sheotar
John Sheoter
Wm Sheoter
Thomas Sheoter
Thos Shepeherd
Ric'd Shepehurd
John Shephard
Ric'd Shepherd
John Shepherd
Rbt. Shephurd

John Shephurd
John Sheppard
John Sheppurd
Thomas Sherwyn
Philip Sherwyn
Jacob Sherwyn
John Sherad
Wm Shete
John Shipster
John Shipster snr
Robert Shipster
Jacob Shoo
William Shoo
John Shooe
John Shorte snr
John Shorte jnr
Thomas Shote
John Shote
Richard Shyppard
John Shypper
Richard Shypper
Agnes Sill
John Skee
William Skee
Thos Skoytte
John Skynner
Walter Slade
John Slade
Wm Smale
John Smale
Thomas Smale
Richard Smale
Edward Smarte
Smith & Lyde
Henry Smith
Wm Smoddyng
Wm Smyth
Walter Smyth
Thos Smyth
Richard Smyth
John Smyth
Thos Smyth
Thomas Smythe
Richard Smythe
John Smythes
George Snell
Robert Snell

R'ch'rd Snell (d) (B)
Snoddeshall
John Snyde
Thos Some
John Somer
Thos Somer
Thos Somerfett
Richard Somers
Wm Somerset
Thos Somersett
Joanna Sommer
John Sonway
Thomas Soote
John Sosse
Wm of Souton Kt
Thomas Sparke snr
Philip Sparke
Thos Sparke
Richard Sparke
John Speke
Richard Spencer
Thos Spencer
Wm Spencer
John Spencer
Wm Spore
Richard Spycer
Thomas Squyar
John Squyar
Richard Srewall
Richard Staunton, vicar.
John Staunton
Agnes Steor
Wm Stephens
John Stephens
John Stere
Thomas Stevyns
Willaim Stocke
John Stocke
Thos Stock (d)
Thos Stocke
Thos Stockeman
John Stokehame
Thos Stokes
Stephen Stoke
John Stone
Stephen Stone
Thos Stone

Occupier

John Store
John Storke (d)
Robert Storke
Wm Stotte
Thos Street
Robert Strete
Richard Strete
John Strete
Alice Strode (w)
Wm Strode
Agnes Styberry (w)
Willliam Style
John Style
Richard Style
Robert Styrtuppe
Robt. Suellyng
Philip Sutton
John Swale
John Swale II
Richard Swale
Thos Swayne (d)
Alice Swete
John Sweteappull
Robert Swyne
Agnes Sykes
Richard Sylling
John Sym jnr
Philip Sym
John Symmes
Wm Symmes
Richard Symmes
Richard Symmys
William Synnes
Thomas Sythe

Joanna Tachell (w)
John Talbatt
Joanna Taneard
Richard Tanner
John Tanner
William Tanner
Thos Taylor
Cornelius Taylor
William Taylor
Isabella Taylor (w)
John Tayllor
Wm Tedbury

John Tedbury
Wm Templer
John Templer
Abb't of T'wk'sb'ry
Joanna Theacher (w)
Henry Thomas (d)
John Thomasse
John Thommasse
John Thomson
Richard Thorne
John Thorne
John Thorneton
Wm Tokersd
Thomas Tolchard
Thomas Tomer
Robert Tommesend
John Tooker
Wm Tooker
Walter Torney
Wm Torney
Margaret Tothyll
Robert Totyn
Richard Touker
Robert Tourney
Cristina Towker (w)
Thomas Towker
John Towler
Wm Tracy
Nicholas Tradbezote
Edward Trapp
Richard Traske
Wm Travell
Thos Trote
Wm Trybody
John Tryman
Wm Tryvett
Wm Tudber
John Tudberd
Wm Tudbere
Wm Tupper
Wiliam Turner
Thos Turner
Walter Turner
John Turner
Agnes Turner
Richard Turrell
Thos Tutber

John Tutbotte
Alice Tutber
John Tuttyn
John Tutyey
John Tyke
Henry Tyler
Nicholas Tyler
Richard Tyler
John Tynkenell
Thos Tyntenhull
Robert Tyntenhull

John Uphyll

John Vagge
John Varie
William Vayce
Thomas Vayle
Wm Vayle
Thomas Veell
Thos Vermyn
John Vesy
Robert Vincent
John Vowles
Wm Vowlys
John Vowelys
Thos Vyterok

Thos Waddon
Joanna Wade
John Wadon
Joanna Walle
John Walle
William Waltes
John Walter
William Walton (B)
John Warde
John Warman
John Warner
John Warren
John Warren
John Warr
John Warren
Richard Warren
John Warwyke
Richard Warwike
John Waryne

William Wason
John Wason
John Wason jnr
Philip Wastell
Wm Wastefold
Edith Wastell (w)
R'ch'rd Waterhouse
John Wathill
John Watkyns
John Watteson
John Wayne
Wm Waywyse
John Webbe
William Webbe
John Webbe (d)
Thos Webbe
George Wele
John Wener
John Wengar
Thos Wengar
Henry Weryng
John Weston (B)
John West
Walter West
Edith West
Henry West
Thos West
Wm West
Wm Weste
John Weste snr
John Weste jnr
Thos Weste
Robert Weston
Thomas Wethall
Henry Weyning
John Whekar
John Wheker
John Whibery
Simon White
Thos White
Thos Whiting
Walt. Whitlock (d)
John Whthy
John Whybery
Thom Whybury
Thos Whyte
John Whyte (d)

Occupier

Wm Whyteputt
John Whytewode
Wm Whyteworde
Thos Whyting (B)
Thos Whyting
Wm Whyting
Alice Whytyng
ThosWibbery
John Wilcock
Henry Willett
Alex Wilmott
John Wimlott
John Withie
Andrew Woderofe
Thos Wodeward
Chr'stin' Wodrove w)
Wm Wodyar
Thos Wolshe
John Worlock
Robert Wrothe (d)
Wm Wrotte
John Wrotte
Richard Wryte
Peter Wyche
John Wyke
Agnes Wyke
Wm Wyke
Edward Wyke
Thos Wylcock
John Wylcocke
Richard Wylkyns
John Wylkyns
John Wyllcocke
John Wylliams
John Wylls (smith)
Wylock & Rooly
Thos Wylock
Wylock & Baker
Wm Wylock
Richard Wylton
Thos Wynscombe
Thos Wynyns
Cecelia Wyrde (w)
John Wyse
Edith Wythy
John Wythy
Thos Wythy

Thos Wythyfield
John Wyther
John Wythys
Edmund Wyxy

Robert Yadlof
Willian Yadoff
William Yadolf
Richard Yalalf
William Yelle
John Ylle
Wm Yockner
John Yong
Wm Yonge
John Yonge
Thos Yonge
John Yonge
Alice Yonge (w)
Wm Yonge
John Yongh
Henry Young
Thos Young
Christina Young
John Young
Wm Yrland

References

[1] B.Harvey. *The Estates of Westminster Abbey.* Oxford University Press (OUP) 1977

[2] The *Valor Ecclesiasticus* was Henry VIII's record of church finances. Compiled in 1535-36, it is a detailed survey and valuation of church property in England and Wales. References to the *Valor* are to the translation by Caley & Hunter. London 1810-34, vol.1 pp 142-147 for the Glastonbury entries

[3] This book is based on translations of the terriers of Abbot Beere. 1515-16. British Library (BL) Egerton MS 3034 and 3134; Harley MS 3961; Society of London Antiquaries MS 653 (Baltonsborough); Mells Manor Muniments (M.M.M.) 36 &37 (Doulting and Mells).

[4] *Victoria County History (VCH) v*ol II, p. 97

[5] VCH ibid. p. 94

[6] A.Savine *Oxford Studies in Social & Legal History v*ol. 1. p. 50

[7] C.R.Routh *Who's Who in Tudor England.* p. 73

[8] Henry Vlll *Letters & Papers* 1540. 809

[9] V C H vol ll ibid.

[10] V C H vol ll ibid.

[11] Bristol Records Office 36074 (88)

[12] Henry Vlll *Letters and Papers* 1540. 809

[13] J.Carley *Glastonbury Abbey, The Holy House,*p.144. Gothic Image 1988

[14] Dugdale*, Monasticon*, p.9

[15] BL cat. p.305

[16] Grittleton terrier p.1

[17] M. Williams, *The Draining of the Somerset Levels* Cambridge, 1970

[18] Sir Williamm.Dugdale Kt. *Monasticon Anglicanum* 1655. Trans. Caley,Ellis & Bandinel. vol.1. London 1817

[19] Margaret McGregor BA Dip. Archive Admin.

[20] M.Bailey *The English Manor* & H.S.Bennett, *Life on the English Manor.* Cambridge 1960

[21] As above and private note from Dr M.G.Thompson

[22] Private note from Barbara Harvey

[23] I. Keil, '*The Estates of the abbey of Glastonbury in the later middle ages*', (University of Bristol, unpublished PhD. thesis, 1964) p. 78.

[24] Personal communication from Dr M.G. Thompson. The present-day farm site can be easily seen from the M5, going south, on the left immediately after crossing the Huntspill River bridge.

[25] Dugdale *Monasticon* p.10

[26] A. Savine, op. cit. vol.1 (1909).

[27] Henry VIII's surveyors, Richard Pollard and Thomas Moyle, carried out a full survey of the Glastonbury estate after the suppression but this survey has

not been traced in full. Parts have been located in the Public Records Office (PRO) and are referenced accordingly. It is clear that Dugdale's *Monasticon Anglicanum* draws extensively on Pollard & Moyle's work. Text references to Dugdale may therefore be understood as references to that transcription of the P&M survey. This was to be completed by December 5th 1539, Richard Pollard reporting to Thomas Cromwell that the 'true value' would follow shortly. *Henry VIII Letters and Papers 1539*, p.637

[28] McGregor op cit.

[29] Dugdale, *Monasticon*, p.11

[30] Dugdale, *Monasticon*, pp.11 & 19

[31] Dugdale, *Monasticon*, up to and including p.21

[32] P.A. Cunich, '*The Administration and Alienation of Ex-monastic Lands by the Crown, 1536-47* (Cambridge University PhD. thesis), p. 148

[33] PRO E/315/420 ff 47 & 48

[34] Dugdale, *Monasticon*, p.11.

[35] Dugdale, *Monasticon*, p.16.

[36] Dom Aldred Watkin, *The Great Cartulary of Glastonbury*, Somerset Record Society (Watkin) vol. III p. ccxi

[37] Dugdale, *Monasticon*, pp. 18 & 19

[38] As above

[39] Watkin. op cit. vol.lll p. ccxv

[40] L. Abrams, *Anglo-Saxon Glastonbury: Church and Endowment* (1996), pp. 107-8. (Abrams)

[41] PRO E/315/420 6938s/f.12

[42] Private communication from Barbara Harvey

[43] Watkin, op cit. vol. III, p.ccxvi

[44] PRO E/315/420/6938/ f.12 & 43.

[45] Watkin, op. cit. vol. III, p.ccxvii; Abrams, op. cit. pp. 132-3.

[46] PRO E/315/420/6938/s

[47] Watkin, op. cit. vol. III, p. ccxxii.

[48] PRO E/315/420/6938/s

[49] See Abrams, op. cit. p. 88 for her view of the quality of this land

[50] Watkin, op. cit. vol. III, p.ccxxv

[51] Watkin, op. cit. vol. III, p.ccxvi; see also Abrams, *op. cit.* pp.149-52 on the origins of the Kington estate.

[52] PRO E/315/420/6938 f.43v.

[53] Watkin, op. cit. vol. III, p. ccxxiv; also Abrams, pp. 249-52

[54] Abrams, pp. 47-9; Watkin, vol. III, p.ccxxix

[55] PRO E/315/420/6938. F.44

[56] Watkin, op. cit. vol. II, p.clxxxi; see also Abrams,op. cit. pp. 69-72 for the origins of the Brent and Lympsham manors

[57] S,Rippon. *Severn Estuary* ISBN 0 7185 0069 5

[58] Watkin, op cit. vol. II, p.clxxxi

[59] Abrams, op cit. pp. 69-72

[60] Watkin, op cit. vol. II, p. clxxxi et seq.

[61] Abrams, op cit. pp. 69-72

[62] Watkin, op cit. vol. II, p clxxxvii; also Abrams, pp. 254-5.

[63] Dugdale *Monasticon* p.12 and PRO E315/420/6938 f.71

[64] Abrams,op cit. pp. 166-7.

[65] Watkin, op cit. vol. II, p.clxxxviii et seq.

[66] Watkin op.cit. vol. II p.clxxxix

[67] Dugdale, *Monasticon*, p.7.

[68] BL. Egerton 3321, ff 105-8 and 119-21

[69] *Valor,* vol. 1, p.145

[70] PRO E/315/420/ 6938/f.71

[71] Watkin, op cit. vol. II, p. clvi

[72] Cunich, op.cit. p.293.

[73] Watkin, op. cit. vol. II, p.cxxxi; also Abrams, pp. 204-11.

[74] If any reader knows the whereabouts of any of these, the author would be pleased to be informed.

[75] Watkin, op. cit. vol. III, p.civ; Abrams, pp. 112-4

[76] PRO E315/420/6938/f.71

[77] Personal communication from Dr M G Thompson. and SNHS 1997 p.103

[78] Watkin, op cit, vol. II, p.cl; also Abrams, pp. 200-4

[79] BL. Egerton 3321

[80] PRO E/315/420/6938/s

[81] Dugdale *Monasticon* p.15

[82] Abrams op cit.

[83] Dugdale *Monasticon*, p.15

[84] Watkin, op. cit. vol. II, p.cxlviii; it is the later work of Abrams which suggests that half of this donation was to *Scobbanwirh* , perhaps later associated with the manor of Ditcheat, Abrams, , pp. 53-4

[85] Dugdale *Monasticon*, p. 14

[86] Watkin, op cit. vol. II, p.cxlviii; Abrams, pp. 76-77

[87] Dugdale *Monasticon*, p. 13

[88] PRO E315/420/6938s f.50

[89] Abrams, op. cit.pp.169-71..

[90] M. Williams, *The Draining of the Somerset Levels* (1970), pp. 105-7

[91] Dugdale *Monasticon*, p. 11 and PRO E/315/420/6938/f41

[92] Abrams, op. cit. p. 131

[93] Dugdale *Monasticon*, p. 12

[94] PRO E/315/420/6938/ f 78

[95] Abrams,op cit. p.218-20

[96] PRO E315/420//6938/ f.55

[97] As above. f40

[98] Abrams,op. cit. pp. 153-4.

[99] Watkin, op cit. vol. II, p. clxviii

[100] PRO E315/420/6938/ f.56

[101] Watkin, op cit. vol. II, p. clx

[102] PRO E315/420/6938/, f.57

[103] Personal communication from Dr M.G. Thompson.

[104] Abrams, op cit. pp. 80-2

[105] PRO E 315/420/6938/f. 53v

[106] Watkin, op. cit. vol. II, p. clxiii et seq; also Abrams, p. 174-5

[107]PRO E344, f52

[108] Dugdale, *Monasticon*, p. 1. For a more recent acount of the origins of the core estate   see Abrams, pp. 123-131

[109] PRO E315/420/6938/, f.79

[110] Dugdale, *Monasticon*, p. 10

[111] BRO 36074 (88)

[112] VCH op. cit.

[113] PRO E315/420/6938/ f. 34

[114] Dugdale *Monasticon*, p. 16.

114 PRO E315/420/6938/, f. 47.

[116] As above f. 37.

[117] Abrams,op cit pp. 155-7.

[118] PRO E 315/420/6938/ f. 68.

[119] As above

[120] N.E. Stacy, '*Henry of Blois and the lordship of Glastonbury*', English Historical Review, February, 1999

End

GLASTONBUF

CW0054747l

Pocket Picture Guides

Limb Injuries

Pocket Picture Guides

Limb Injuries

Peter Burge FRCS
Consultant Orthopaedic Surgeon,
John Radcliffe Hospital,
Oxford, UK.

J.B. Lippincott Company • Philadelphia •
Gower Medical Publishing • London • New York

Distributed in USA and Canada by:
J.B. Lippincott Company
East Washington Square
Philadelphia, PA 19105
USA

Distributed in UK and Continental Europe by:
Harper & Row Ltd
Middlesex House
34-42 Cleveland Street
London W1P 5FB
UK

**Distributed in Philippines/Guam, Middle East,
Latin America and Africa by:**
Harper & Row International
East Washington Square
Philadelphia, PA 19105
USA

**Distributed in Southeast Asia, Hong Kong,
India and Pakistan by:**
Harper & Row Publishers (Asia) Pte Ltd
37 Jalan Pemimpin 02-01
Singapore 2057

Distributed in Japan by:
Igaku Shoin Ltd
Tokyo International
P.O. Box 5063
Tokyo
Japan

Distributed in Australia and New Zealand by:
Harper & Row (Australasia) Pty Ltd
P.O. Box 226
Artarmon, N.S.W. 2064
Australia

Library of Congress Catalog Number: 87-82131

British Library Cataloguing in Publication Data

Burge, Peter
    Limb injuries.
    I. Man. Limbs. Injuries
    I. Title II. Series
    617'.58044

ISBN: 0-397-44576-8 (Lippincott/Gower)

Project Editor: Michele Campbell
Design: Nigel Duffield

Produced by Mandarin Offset/
Printed in Hong Kong in 1989

ACKNOWLEDGEMENTS

The author is grateful to Mr Nigel Henderson FRCS and Mr Gregory Houghton FRCS who kindly provided illustrations for this book.

CONTENTS

Introduction

Limb injury is a serious cause of disability, especially in the young victims of motorcycle and other road accidents. Whilst the management of injuries to the trunk and head rightly takes priority, the primary management of limb injuries is of great importance, since it is injury to the limbs which usually determines the final disability. If limb injuries are given low priority, the time for optimum treatment may be missed and the prospect of regaining good limb function lost forever.

This book attempts to present a logical approach to the injured limb, using pictures supplemented by diagrams and tables where appropriate. It concentrates on common injuries but includes some less common ones which require prompt recognition and treatment. The first part of the book deals with the assessement and management of injury to each tissue within the limb. The second section covers injury to the various parts of the upper and lower limbs. Injuries to the hand are covered in another book in this series, though some hand injuries are used here to illustrate principles which apply to limb injury in general.

Most injured patients presenting to hospital in Great Britain are seen first by relatively inexperienced medical staff. It is hoped that this book will help those in the front line of trauma management to recognize serious limb injury, to beware of some common pitfalls and, perhaps most important, to know when more experienced or specialist help should be sought.

Assessment

The first responsibility of the doctor treating limb injury is to ensure that no life-threatening injury is present. The injured limb seldom represents immediate danger to the patient, but it is often associated with damage to the axial skeleton and viscera. Attention should first be directed to these areas, and only when the ABC of

Airway	Breathing	Circulation

are under control, should examination of the limb proceed.

History

A history must be obtained whenever possible. Although the dramatic appearance of the injured limb may invite immediate examination, the physician must resist this temptation. The history may elicit vital information which cannot be obtained by other means and should never be omitted.

The mechanism of injury will often indicate the nature, extent and severity of trauma and may alert the doctor to the presence of unexpected problems. Furthermore, the patient's occupation, general health and social circumstances may influence his management and response to treatment. Finally, the history-taking enables the examiner to gain the patient's confidence and to provide reassurance.

Physical Examination

In many limb injuries, a fracture or wound is immediately apparent. Evidence of damage to vessel, nerve, tendon and joint may be much less obvious and injuries to these structures are often overlooked at the first examination. The opportunity for optimum treatment of such injuries may be lost and the outcome jeopardized if diagnosis and treatment are delayed. Nerve palsy may be wrongly attributed to treatment (and the doctor blamed) unless the initial examination is performed thoroughly and carefully recorded.

Errors in diagnosis usually result simply from failure to consider the possibility of, for example, nerve injury or from failure to perform the appropriate straightforward clinical tests. The only safe rule is to assume that a structure is damaged until proved otherwise.

> If a limb is lacerated,
> **all** the structures in the limb
> should be presumed to be injured
> **until proved otherwise** by either:
>
> 1. Adequate clinical examination
> or
> 2. Surgical exploration.

A systematic approach to examination of the limb will usually lead to an accurate assessment of the injury.

Cutaneous Injury

Mechanism of injury	Tissue damage
Incised wound	+
Puncture wound	+ +
Laceration	+ +
Shear wound	+ + + +
Crush wound	+ + + + +
Missile wound	variable

Fig. 1 Classification of wounds. The classification which most accurately reflects the extent of tissue damage is based upon the mechanism of injury.

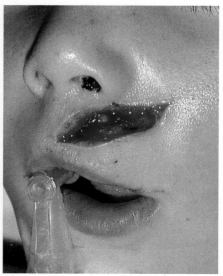

Fig. 2 Incised wound. The wound edges are clean and tidy, resemble a surgical incision and bleed freely. The adjacent skin is pink with brisk capillary refill.

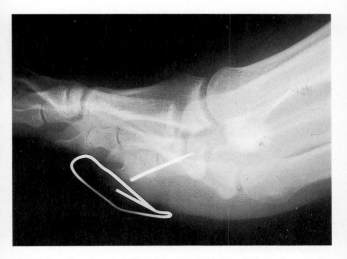

Fig. 3 Puncture wound. The entry wound is small. An exit wound may or may not be present; the wounding agent may still impale the tissues. Needles often break beneath the surface, leaving the tip in the limb. Removal from the sole of the foot is deceptively difficult and often requires general anaesthesia, tourniquet and image intensifier. Removal of a needle should not be attempted under local anaesthesia unless it can be seen or felt.

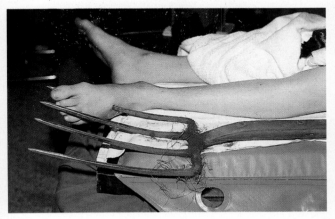

Fig. 4 Puncture wounds may become infected, particularly in the foot. The treatment is wound cleansing, elevation and rest. A prophylactic antibiotic is usually given but will not prevent infection unless the limb is also elevated and rested, preferably by immobilization in a plaster slab.

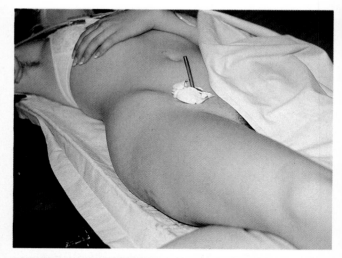

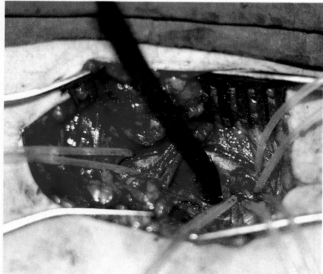

Fig. 5 Large foreign bodies which impale the limb near major vessels should be left in place until the patient is in the operating room and removed only when proximal control of the vessels has been obtained. This girl (upper) fell on a fishing-rod stand which pierced the groin and emerged in the buttock. The femoral artery was displaced (lower) but was fortunately uninjured.

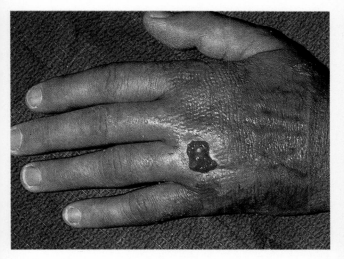

Fig. 6 Bites (animal or human) on the limbs have a high risk of infection and should be left open. This man has septic arthritis of a metacarpophalangeal joint after suture of a human tooth wound.

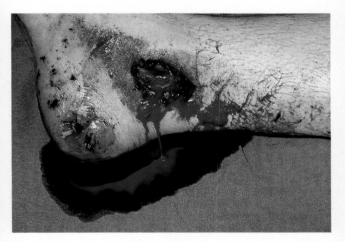

Fig. 7 Laceration. The skin has either been cut with an irregular object or torn, producing a ragged wound with a variable amount of damage to its edges. The wound edges should be trimmed back to uninjured tissue.

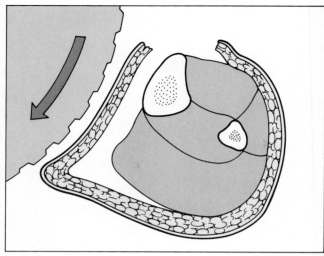

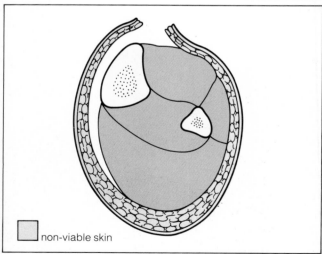

non-viable skin

Fig. 8 Shear injury. A tangential shear force strips the skin from the deep fascia, tearing the vessels which supply the skin. Large areas of skin may be non-viable. The wound edges appear white or dusky with no marginal bleeding. Capillary refill is poor or absent. Extensive necrosis may occur, especially if the lesion is not recognized and is managed by direct suture.

Fig. 9 The ring handle of a surgical instrument, pressed onto the skin and then released, will demonstrate capillary refill of the resulting ring of pallor and is a useful test in pale skin. Refill should be compared with the corresponding area of the opposite limb.

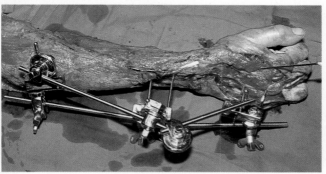

Fig. 10 The skin may be stripped completely from the limb (degloving). This arm was caught between the road and a car that rolled, sparing only the skin of the palm and fingers.

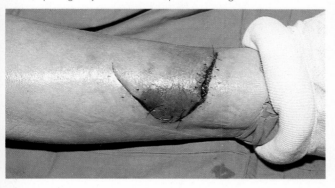

Fig. 11 A common shear injury affects the elderly female shin, where the skin is thin and fragile. A triangular flap is raised, usually based distally. Its arterial inflow is poor and the venous drainage worse. Sutures place tension on the skin, decrease its perfusion and often lead to necrosis of the entire flap. Dead skin should be excised and the flap held in place without tension using adhesive strips. Healing may be delayed. Large, non-viable flaps should be excised and a skin graft applied primarily.

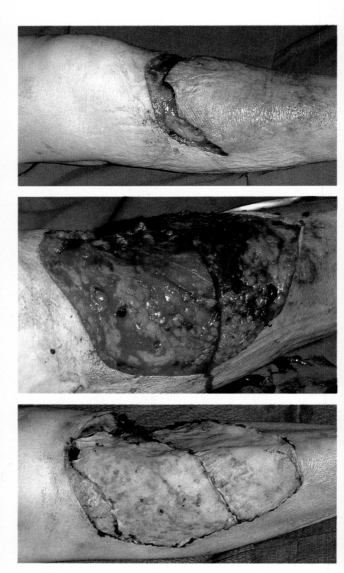

Fig. 12 A large shear injury on the shin of an elderly lady (upper). Non-viable skin was excised (middle) and the area was covered by a split skin graft (lower).

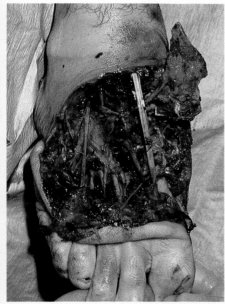

Fig. 13 Crush injury. The size of the wound may give little indication of the severity of damage to the skin and muscle. Release of myoglobin from crushed muscle may cause renal failure. Gas gangrene may occur if non-viable muscle is not excised promptly.

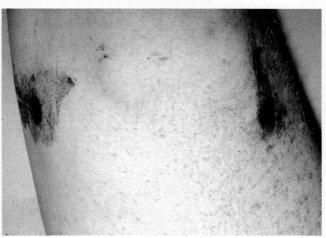

Fig. 14 Missile wound. Low-velocity missiles (hand guns, low-velocity rifles) cause relatively little tissue damage, although structures in the direct path of the projectile may be injured. Both entry and exit wounds are small. Removal of the bullet is indicated only if it lies within a joint or is easily accessible.

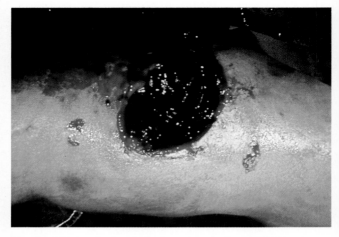

Fig. 15 A high-velocity missile (muzzle velocity>2,000 ft/sec) creates a pressure wave which destroys a cylinder of tissue along its path. The exit wound is large. Missile wounds should never be treated by primary closure because of the risk of infection.

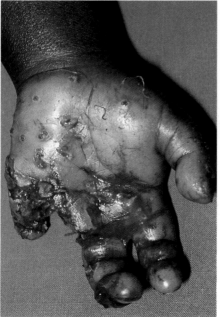

Fig. 16 Close-range shotgun wounds may remove large areas of tissue, but it is usually impossible to remove all the pellets. This 2-year-old child was caught in the cross-fire of a domestic feud.

Vascular Injury

Collateral vessels cannot be relied upon in the injured limb. In the limb affected by peripheral vascular disease, viability of the distal segment is often maintained by perfusion through collateral vessels. In acute injury, however, there is no time for the enlargement of collaterals and these vessels may be compromised by injury or by swelling of the tissues they traverse. For example, popliteal artery injuries frequently cause distal gangrene, whereas an atherosclerotic lesion at the same level usually does not. Untreated vascular injuries lead to gangrene.

Vessels may be injured by:

1. compression

2. laceration

3. rupture (complete or intimal)

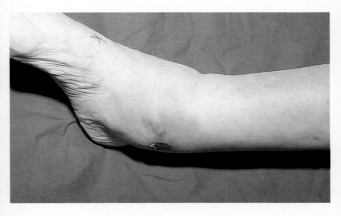

Fig. 17 Compression. Severe displacement of a fracture or dislocation may compress or kink vessels and cause ischaemia. In addition, skin viability may be threatened by pressure from under-lying bone fragments. Urgent reduction of the fracture is required. If the fracture is closed, reduction may be performed under sedation at the time of first examination. Reduction and stabilization of displaced fractures, together with restoration of circulating volume, will usually restore perfusion of the extremity. If not, vascular injury should be assumed until proved otherwise, either by arteriography or exploration of the vessel in question.

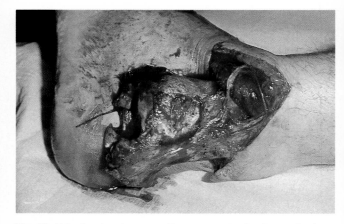

Fig. 18 If the fracture is open with gross contamination, reduction of the exposed bone will carry organisms into the limb (where they are much more difficult to remove) and should not be performed in the accident department. Patients presenting with distal ischaemia should be taken urgently to the operating theatre, where the fragments are cleaned and irrigated before returning them to their normal position.

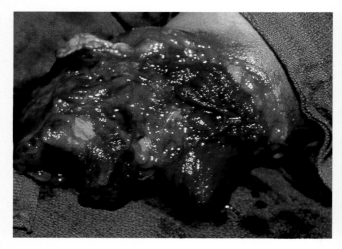

Fig. 19 Laceration. The muscular walls of completely severed arteries retract and bleeding often stops spontaneously. This forearm was amputated in a farm machine but there was little bleeding. However, a partially divided artery cannot retract and the bleeding may be difficult to control.

Fig. 20 Methods for control of bleeding. Ligation of the vessel stump is more difficult than it sounds. Adjacent nerves and tendons may be damaged inadvertently. It should not be used in the hand. Note that a tourniquet is hazardous and very seldom necessary or justified.

Fig. 21 Rupture. Closed injury may rupture the entire vessel and produce a rapidly-expanding haematoma. Here, rupture of the femoral artery accompanied a fracture of the femur.

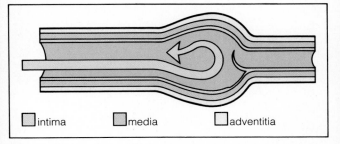

☐ intima   ☐ media   ☐ adventitia

Fig. 22 Often only the intima (the least elastic layer) is torn. An intimal flap may occlude the lumen and lead to thrombus formation at the site of injury. This common lesion is sometimes erroneously interpreted as 'spasm', but 'spasm' should never be accepted as an explanation for limb ischaemia.

15

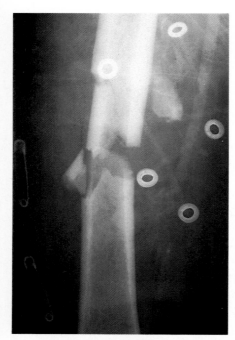

Fig. 23 This femoral artery was injured at the level of a fracture.

Fig. 24 The injured segment of vessel was contused, narrowed and non-pulsatile. It contained an intimal flap tear. Excision of the segment and reconstruction by direct repair or, more often, by reversed vein graft, as shown here (arrowed), is required.

16

Physical signs of vascular injury

Pallor
Absent capillary refill
Decreased temperature
Diminished distal pulses
Empty veins
Paralysis (late sign)

Fig. 25 Physical signs of vascular injury. Diminished distal pulses may be difficult to feel in a swollen limb. Doppler examination may help.

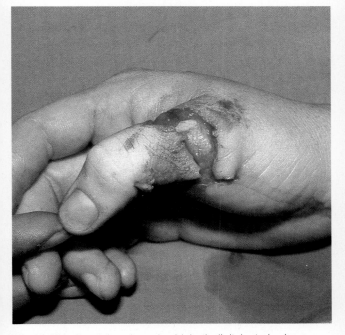

Fig. 26 This thumb is pale and cold: both digital arteries have been divided and need repair.

Muscular Injury

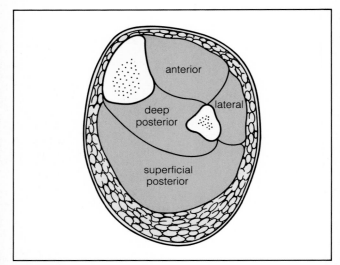

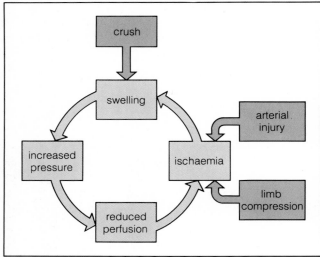

Fig.27 Compartment syndrome. In both the upper and lower limb, several muscle groups lie within relatively unyielding osseofascial compartments, for example anterior tibial (upper) and anterior forearm. If, for any reason, the pressure within a compartment exceeds the perfusion pressure, muscle and nerve ischaemia result. Ischaemic muscle swells and a cycle of increasing swelling, pressure and ischaemia may occur (lower).

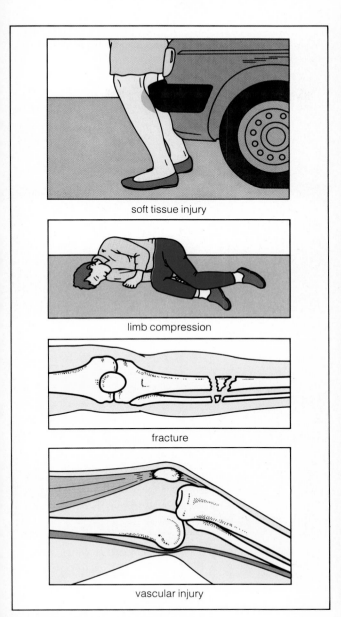

soft tissue injury

limb compression

fracture

vascular injury

Fig. 28 Causes of compartment syndrome.

Fig. 29 Raised compartment pressure: predisposing factors.

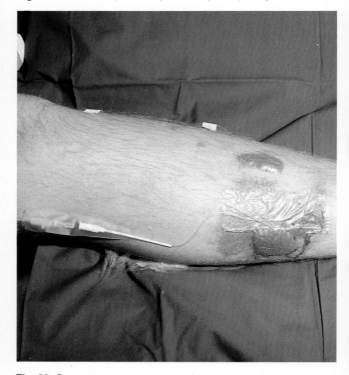

Fig. 30 Compartment pressure may be measured simply by means of a 'slit' catheter placed in the compartment through a wide-bore needle and connected by saline-filled tubing to a pressure recorder. Four 2mm longitudinal slits in the catheter tip prevent occlusion by the tissues. A pressure of 60 mmHg was recorded in the deep posterior compartment 12 hours after a tibial fracture sustained in a motorcycle accident.

Compartment syndrome

Symptoms: **severe pain**, out of proportion to the injury
paraesthesiae

Signs: tense limb
pain on passive stretch of affected muscles
neurological abnormality

Test: compartment pressure measurement

Treatment: remove encircling dressings/casts
release fascia throughout length of
compartment

Fig. 31 Compartment syndrome.

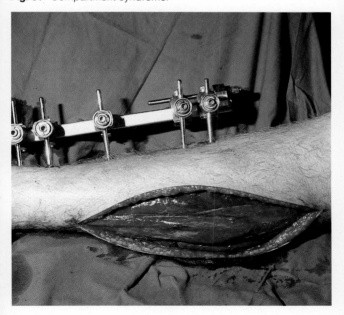

Fig. 32 Fasciotomy of all four compartments in the leg. Note the
bulging of swollen but viable muscle into the wound.

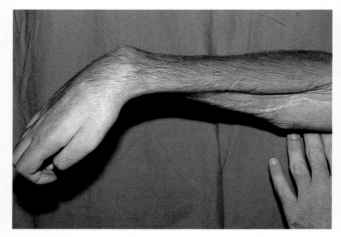

Fig. 33 Volkmann's contracture is the result of untreated compartment syndrome in the flexor forearm compartment.

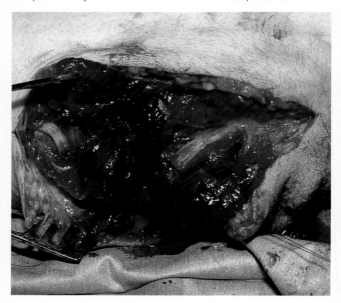

Fig. 34 Laceration. Lacerated muscle heals with a short segment of scar and the disability which results depends upon the amount of muscle damage. Here, the flexor carpi ulnaris muscle and the ulnar nerve were cut on a sheet of glass.

Tendon Injury

Fig. 35 Causes of tendon injury.

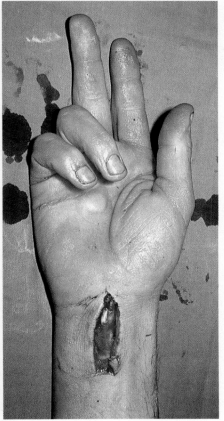

Fig. 36 Laceration of the flexor tendons of the index and middle fingers is indicated by the extended posture of these digits.

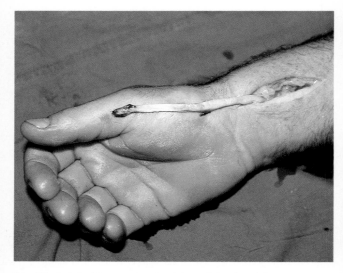

Fig. 37 A violent hyperextension injury of the thumb has caused traumatic rupture of the flexor pollicis longus tendon at its insertion.

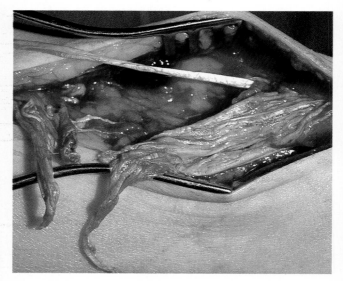

Fig. 38 Rupture of a degenerate Achilles tendon occurs in middle-aged athletes. Note the frayed ends of the tendon. The plantaris tendon was also ruptured.

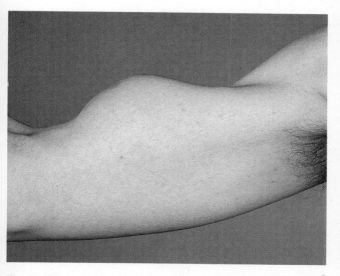

Fig. 39 Rupture of the tendon of the long head of biceps results in a swelling in the arm but little loss of strength.

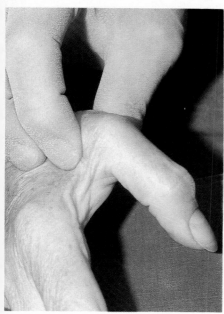

Fig. 40 The extensor pollicis longus tendon may rupture because of attrition over a fracture of the distal radius.

Nerve Injury

Classification of nerve injury		
Type of injury	Extent of injury	Causes of injury
Neurapraxia	conduction block	compression fractures
Axonotmesis	axons disrupted, nerve sheath intact	fractures dislocations
Neurotmesis	axons and sheath disrupted	laceration traction ischaemia

Fig. 41 Classification of nerve injury.

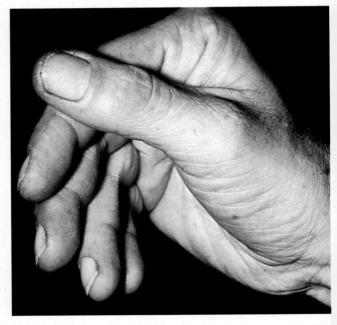

Fig. 42 A rope caught around the elbow caused neurapraxia of the posterior interosseous nerve. Note the inability to extend the metacarpophalangeal joints. Recovery occurred within six weeks.

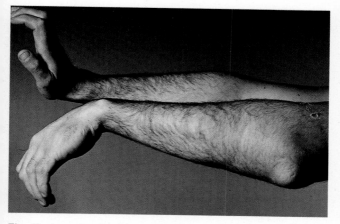

Fig. 43 Axonotmesis of the radial nerve at the site of a humeral fracture. Note the wrist and finger drop. Recovery occurred spontaneously.

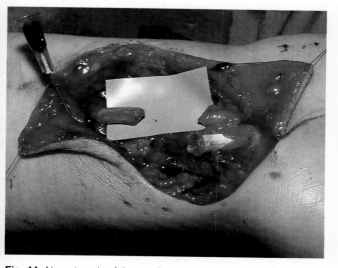

Fig. 44 Neurotmesis of the median nerve due to laceration on glass. If the palmaris longus tendon has been divided, there is a 90% chance that the median nerve is also injured. Primary nerve suture is indicated only if the facilities, skills and time are available for microsurgical repair. If not, it is best to irrigate and close the wound and arrange for an appropriate referral. No harm results from a few days delay.

Fig. 45 Traction injury of the brachial plexus typically occurs in motorcyclists. In this case the radial, musculocutaneous, axillary and medial forearm cutaneous nerves were ruptured at the shoulder. There is extensive damage to the radial nerve (on the left). The axillary artery was also ruptured. These injuries can be repaired by nerve graft with the prospect of some recovery. Often, however, the nerve roots are avulsed from the spinal cord and repair is impossible.

Diagnosis of nerve injury

Motor:	posture
	paralysis
	wasting (after 2-3 weeks)
Sensory:	touch, 2-point discrimination
	pain
Autonomic:	absent sweating

Fig. 46 Diagnosis of nerve injury. Closed nerve palsies quite often remain undetected for some while after injury. They may be wrongly attributed to treatment unless documented accurately at the first examination.

Joint Injury

Types of joint injury

Open wound

Ligament injury

Dislocation

Articular fracture

Fig. 47 Joint injury.

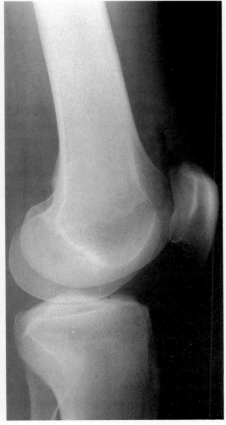

Fig. 48 Penetration of a joint may be revealed by the presence of air on X-ray, in this case in the suprapatellar pouch.

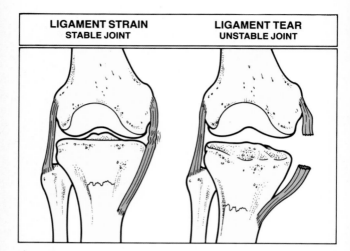

| LIGAMENT STRAIN | LIGAMENT TEAR |
| STABLE JOINT | UNSTABLE JOINT |

Fig. 49 Ligament injury may be partial or complete. Partial injuries cause pain but the joint is stable. Complete ruptures cause joint laxity and the patient may later suffer from instability. Complete ruptures are often less painful than partial tears because the pain receptors in the torn ligament are not stressed by movement and because the haemarthrosis can escape through the torn ligament into the soft tissues. Some ligament ruptures are best treated by early surgical repair (knee, ulnar collateral ligament of thumb metacarpophalangeal joint), so every injured joint should be examined for laxity.

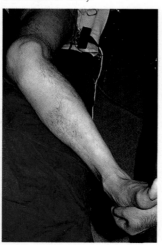

Fig. 50 If the joint is painful, laxity may be masked by muscle spasm and examination under anaesthesia may be necessary to exclude ligament rupture. There is gross valgus laxity in this knee, in which the medial collateral and both cruciate ligaments were ruptured.

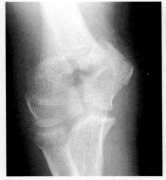
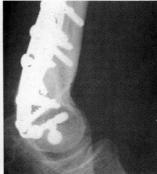

Fig. 51 Articular fractures must be reduced accurately. A few millimetres displacement makes the surfaces incongruous and may cause degenerative arthritis. Displaced joint fractures usually need open reduction and internal fixation, as in this condylar fracture of the distal humerus.

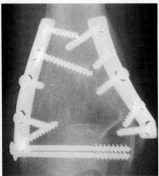

Bone Injury

Causes of fracture	
Trauma:	acute
	repetitive
Pathological:	osteoporosis
	osteomalacia
	tumour
	osteogenesis imperfecta

Fig. 52 Causes of fracture.

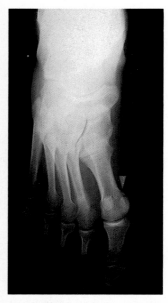

Fig. 53 Stress fracture of the second metatarsal neck (march fracture). Note the cloud of callus (arrowed).

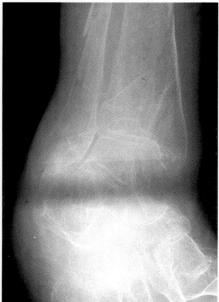

Fig. 54 Fracture of a distal tibia affected by senile osteoporosis.

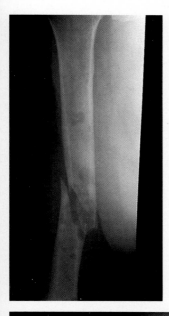

Fig. 55 Pathological fracture of a humerus affected by myeloma.

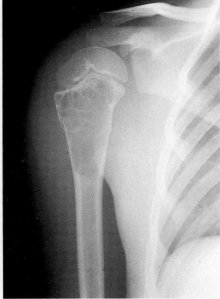

Fig. 56 In children, pathological fracture may occur through a simple bone cyst.

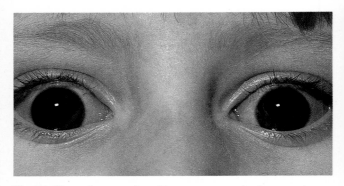

Fig. 57 Blue sclerae are found in some cases of osteogenesis imperfecta.

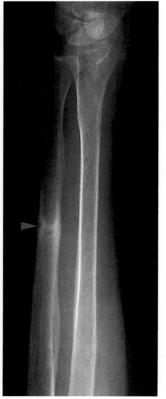

Fig. 58 Looser's zone of the ulna (arrowed) in osteomalacia.

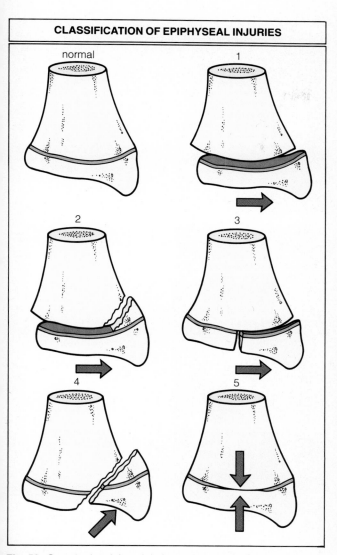

CLASSIFICATION OF EPIPHYSEAL INJURIES

normal

1

2

3

4

5

Fig. 59 Growth plate injury. Injuries to the growth plate are common in children. Five types are recognized. The most frequent is type 2, in which the growing cells of the epiphysis are undamaged. Type 4 usually requires open reduction and internal fixation. Type 5 is often recognized only when premature fusion of the epiphyseal plate occurs.

Shoulder and Arm

Shoulder

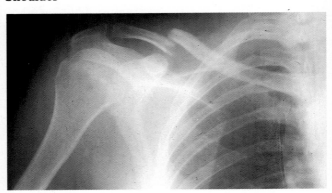

Fig. 60 Fracture of the clavicle is a frequent injury which results from a fall on the limb. Rest in a sling and early movement almost always give union and excellent function, although some deformity is often present over the fracture.

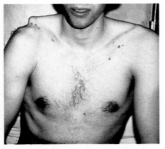

Fig. 61 In acromioclavicular dislocation the strong conoid and trapezoid ligaments which hold the corocoid process to the clavicle are torn. The scapula drops inferiorly, leaving the outer end of the clavicle prominent. Simple use of a sling usually gives good shoulder function, although the prominence tends to persist.

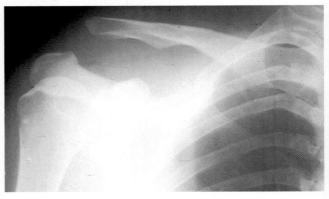

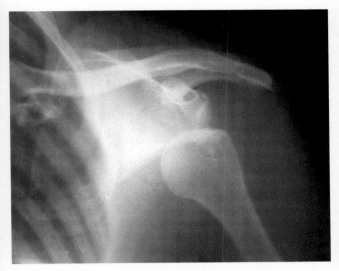

Fig. 62 Anterior dislocation of the shoulder results from an abduction or external rotation injury which tears the anterior capsule. The humeral head is displaced anteriorly and inferiorly. The axillary nerve may be injured. There is a risk of recurrent dislocation, especially in patients under 25 years of age.

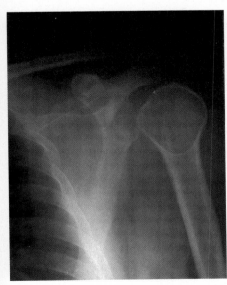

Fig. 63 Posterior dislocation of the shoulder is rare and may be caused by an epileptic fit or an electric shock. The dislocation is directly posterior and may not be obvious on the anteroposterior radiograph, as shown here. A lateral view will confirm that the humeral head is displaced posteriorly.

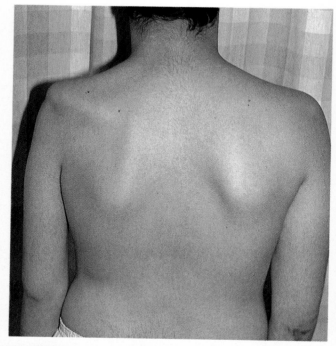

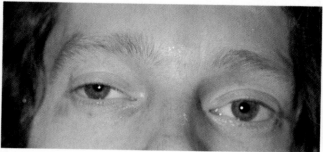

Fig. 64 Injury to the brachial plexus occurs due to traction at the root of the limb. Note the wasting of the scapular muscles and deltoid (upper). There may be an associated vascular injury. The nerves may be damaged anywhere along the course of the plexus, but unfortunately avulsion of the roots from the spinal cord is common and does not recover. Horner's sign (lower) indicates avulsion of the T1 root. If the nerves are ruptured within the plexus itself, nerve grafting may lead to some recovery, especially in the shoulder and elbow muscles.

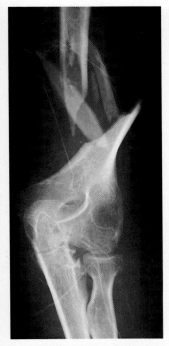

Fig. 65 Humeral shaft fractures may injure the radial nerve as it winds around the bone in the spiral groove.

Fig. 66 Rupture of the long head of the biceps results from attrition of the tendon within the shoulder. Freed from its proximal insertion, the muscle forms a bulge in the arm but there is little weakness because the brachialis and brachioradialis muscles and the short head of the biceps remain intact.

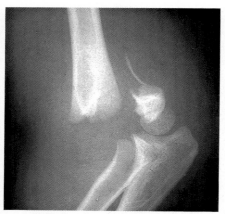

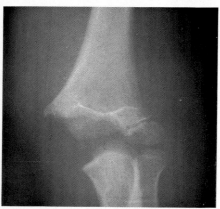

Fig. 67 A supracondylar fracture of the humerus in a child. The brachial artery may be injured or compressed at the elbow, leading to compartment syndrome (see Fig. 27) and Volkmann's ischaemic contracture (Fig. 33). Frequent examination and recording of the circulation, neurological state and ability to extend the fingers is necessary. This fracture requires the attention of an experienced orthopaedic surgeon. Manipulation should be undertaken promptly, before swelling makes reduction difficult.

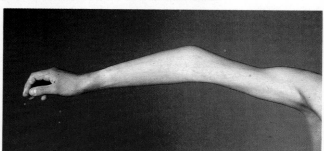

Fig. 68 Malunion of a supracondylar fracture may cause a 'gun-stock' deformity.

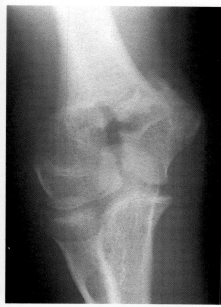

Fig. 69 In adults fractures of the distal humerus often involve the joint surface (upper), necessitating open reduction and internal fixation (lower).

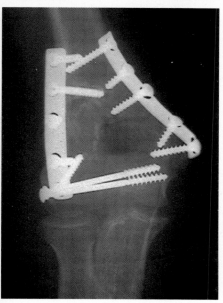

Elbow and Forearm

Elbow Injuries in Children

Fractures are easy to miss in the child's elbow. Much of the skeleton is cartilage and there are several ossific centres which can cause confusion. The exact age at which each centre appears is variable but the order of their appearance is constant (CRITE):

- Capitellum
- Radial head
- Internal (medial) epicondyle
- Trochlea
- External (lateral) epicondyle

A radiograph of the opposite elbow will often be useful for comparison. If the joint is painful, and especially if it is swollen after an injury, a fracture should be strongly suspected. If the periarticular fat lines are displaced, that suspicion approaches certainty.

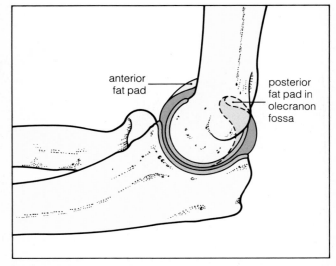

Fig. 70 Periarticular fat is normally visible on a lateral radiograph just anterior to the humeral condyles. A posterior pad of fat is also present but is not seen because it lies in the olecranon fossa (left).

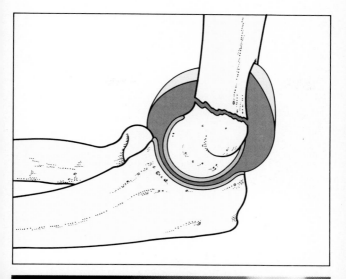

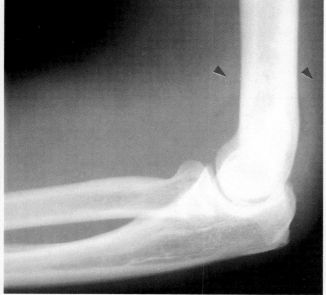

If an articular fracture is present, the haemarthrosis pushes both fat pads away from the humerus and the posterior pad becomes visible (upper and lower).

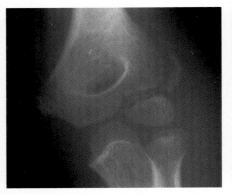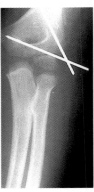

Fig. 71 Fracture of the lateral condyle of the humerus involves a large but partly cartilaginous fragment. If displacement is modest, a small metaphyseal flake of bone may be the only obvious sign of injury (left). However, comparison with a radiograph of the opposite elbow may show that the ossific centre is displaced. Open reduction and fixation (right) is usually necessary to prevent malunion and valgus deformity, which may later cause irritation of the ulnar nerve.

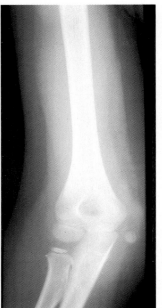

Fig. 72 The medial humeral epicondyle is avulsed by valgus injury of the elbow and may lie some way distal to its normal position. If the elbow dislocates, the epicondyle may be trapped inside the joint after reduction. This possibility should be considered if the epicondyle cannot be seen on the anteroposterior radiograph but is present on the opposite side.

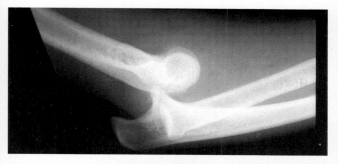

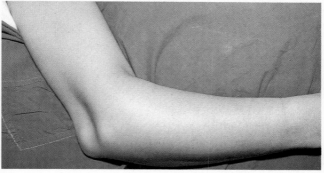

Fig. 73 Dislocation of the elbow is usually posterolateral. The olecranon and radial head are abnormally prominent posteriorly.

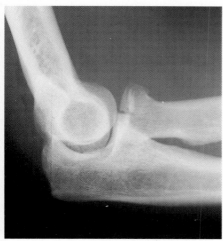

Fig. 74 The radial head is usually broken by a fall on the outstretched hand. The fracture may be visible only on oblique X-rays. Simple fractures are treated by aspiration of the haemarthrosis (for pain relief), rest in a sling and early movement. Severely comminuted fractures are best treated by excision of the radial head.

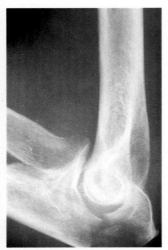

Fig. 75 The olecranon is usually broken by a fall onto the point of the elbow. Displaced fractures need internal fixation to restore continuity of the extensor mechanism and alignment of the joint surface.

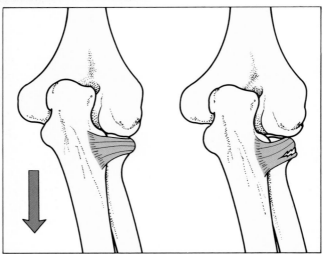

Fig. 76 Pulled elbow is an injury of toddlers produced by traction (blue arrow) on the limb, for example during dressing. A partial tear of the annular ligament permits subluxation of the radial head and a portion of the ligament is trapped in the joint. There is pain, loss of function (suggesting a nerve injury) and the limb is held pronated. The X-rays are normal. Gentle supination of the forearm often produces a click and immediate recovery. If this fails, spontaneous recovery usually occurs in a few days.

Forearm

Fractures of the shafts of the forearm bones are common in both adults and children. Closed reduction and cast treatment is almost always adequate in children. In adults, internal fixation is usually employed because the bones are difficult to control in plaster and any malunion may impair forearm rotation.

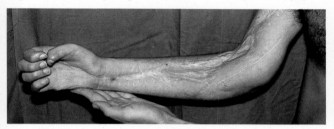

Fig. 77 Volkmann's ischaemic contracture, which developed due to compartment syndrome in a crushed forearm (see Fig. 33).

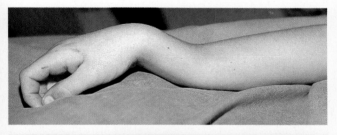

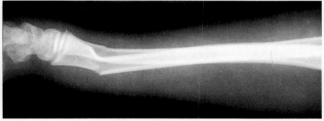

Fig. 78 Diagnosis of fracture of the shafts of the forearm bones is usually obvious because of the deformity (upper), as in this child who broke both bones of the distal forearm. Incomplete ('greenstick') fractures occur in the soft bones of children (lower). Although a single forearm bone may be broken by a direct blow ('nightstick fracture'), fracture of the radius or ulna alone may be associated with a dislocation at the elbow or wrist. The X-rays must show the whole forearm.

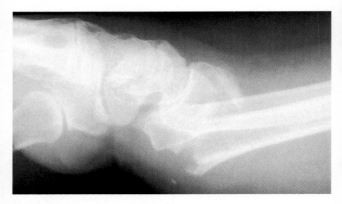

Fig. 79 Colles' fracture occurs when a fall on the outstretched hand, usually in an elderly female, breaks the radius just proximal to the wrist. The 'dinner-fork' deformity comprises dorsal displacement, dorsal angulation and radial deviation of the distal fragment. Closed reduction and plaster immobilization usually give satisfactory results in the elderly.

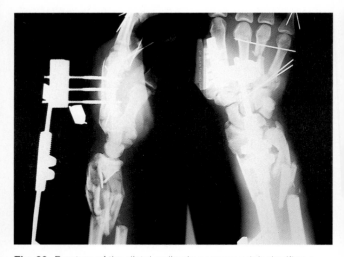

Fig. 80 Fracture of the distal radius in a young adult signifies a much more violent injury than in the elderly osteoporotic wrist. Often there is severe comminution and special care is required to maintain the length of the radius and its relationship to the distal ulna, for example by external skeletal fixation, as seen in this case.

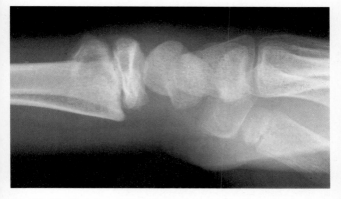

Fig. 81 Fracture-separation of the distal radial epiphysis is a common injury in childhood. The epiphysis itself is undamaged and manipulative reduction is followed by normal growth.

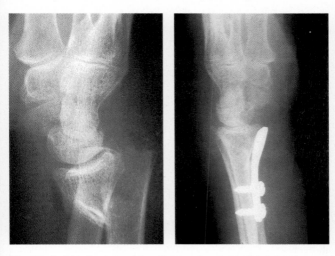

Fig. 82 Smith's fracture of the distal radius (left). This injury is sometimes mistaken for the more common Colles' fracture: remember that the position of the thumb metacarpal indicates which is the anterior surface of the radius. The oblique fracture line allows the distal fragment to slip anteriorly and proximally and it is difficult to hold in plaster. Open reduction and plating is usually necessary (right).

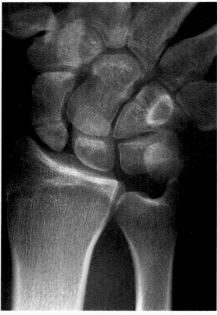

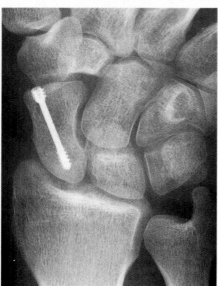

Fig. 83 A scaphoid fracture is caused by a dorsiflexion force and occurs in young adults. There is tenderness and fullness in the anatomical snuff box with limited and painful wrist movements. This clinical picture should be treated by a scaphoid cast, even if X-rays appear normal, for the fracture may not be visible until two weeks after injury. Most undisplaced scaphoid fractures unite after eight weeks in a cast. Fractures which are widely displaced, slow to unite (upper) or associated with carpal dislocation are best treated by internal fixation (lower).

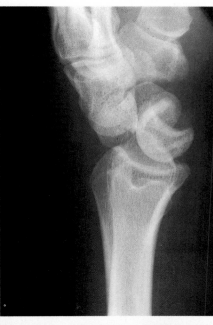

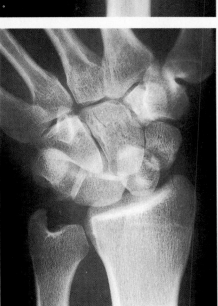

Fig. 84 Carpal dislocation. A history of a heavy fall and the finding of a painful swollen wrist should suggest the possibility of carpal dislocation. There are several types, but the key to diagnosis is the lateral radiograph which shows the carpus displaced (usually dorsally) with respect to the radius (upper). In this case the carpus has dislocated backwards off the lunate. The median nerve may be compressed. These injuries are often missed on the anteroposterior radiograph (lower): comparison with a film of the opposite wrist is helpful.

Hip and Thigh

Hip

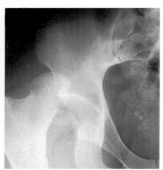

Fig. 85 Dislocation of the hip is usually posterior and may be associated with a fracture of the acetabular rim or sciatic nerve palsy. The limb is held flexed and internally rotated. The dislocation should be reduced as soon as possible to minimize the risk of damage to the blood supply of the femoral head.

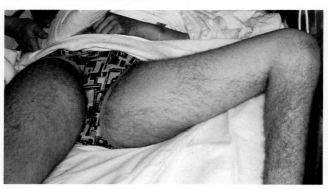

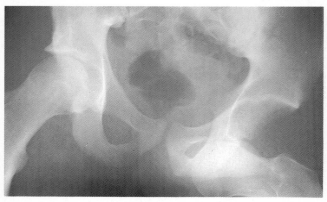

Fig. 86 Anterior dislocation of the hip is less common. The limb is abducted and externally rotated.

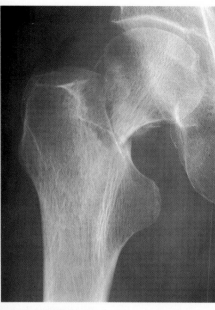

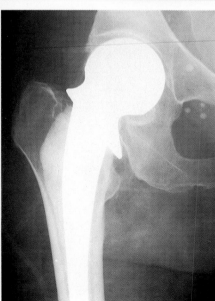

Fig. 87 Fracture of the femoral neck (upper) occurs frequently in the elderly, who are osteoporotic and fall easily. If the fracture is displaced, the limb is shortened and externally rotated. The main complication is osteonecrosis of the femoral head, resulting from injury to the vessels which run along the femoral neck. Operative treatment by internal fixation or prosthetic replacement (lower), followed by immediate mobilization, is the best means of maintaining the elderly patient's activity.

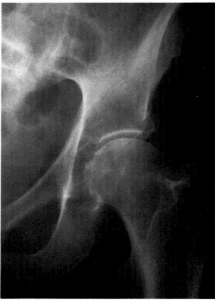

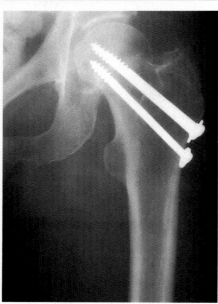

Fig. 88 Undisplaced femoral neck fractures (upper) present with hip pain and a limp. The fracture may displace after a few days or weeks, making treatment more difficult and increasing the risk of osteonecrosis. Undisplaced fractures should, therefore, be stabilized by internal fixation (lower).

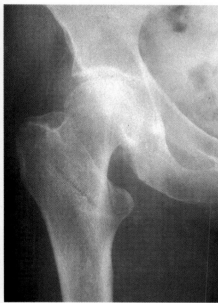

Fig. 89 Trochanteric fractures of the femur (upper) also occur mainly in the aged. The limb is shortened and externally rotated. Reduction and fixation using a sliding screw-plate device (lower) usually permits walking on the day after operation.

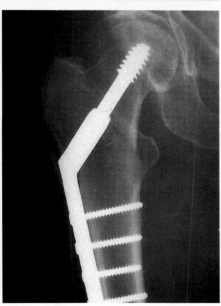

Thigh

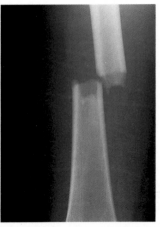

Fig. 90 Fracture of the femoral shaft commonly results from road accidents. The thigh is swollen, deformed, tender and shortened. Immediate management consists of traction and fluid replacement. The thigh can accomodate a large haematoma and blood transfusion is usually needed.

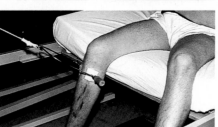

Fig. 91 Skeletal traction through a tibial pin maintains length and alignment of the limb (upper). Perkin's method of traction in a special bed maintains knee movement (middle and lower). When callus appears and some stability is present, a hinged cast-brace will control the fracture and allow mobilization.

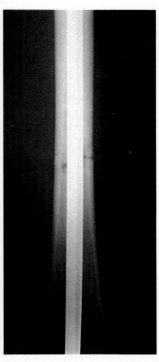

Fig. 92 In some cases, and especially if there are multiple injuries, the fracture is stabilized by closed intramedullary nailing, performed under X-ray control through an incision above the greater trochanter.

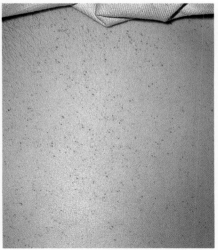

Fig. 93 Fat embolism may occur after a long bone fracture. The patient is confused due to hypoxaemia. Petechiae may be found on the chest wall and axillae. Treatment is directed at maintaining adequate oxygenation, if necessary by ventilation.

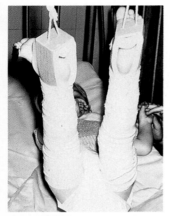

Fig. 94 Femoral shaft fractures in children are usually spiral, resulting from a twisting force. Union occurs promptly with gallow's traction (patients under 2 years old), as seen here, or with skin traction in a Thomas' splint (patients over 2 years old).

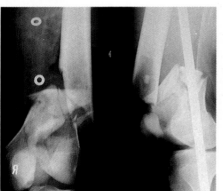

Fig. 95 Fractures of the distal femur which involve displacement of the joint surface need open reduction and internal fixation. The goal is anatomical reduction and rigid fixation, which allows early movement and return of function.

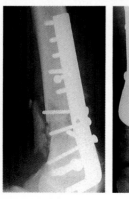

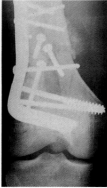

Knee and Leg

Knee

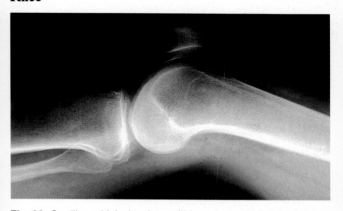

Fig. 96 Swelling which develops within an hour of injury is due to an acute haemarthrosis. If the blood contains fat droplets, an articular fracture must have occurred; further X-rays may be required to demonstrate it. Here, the fat/blood interface is visible in the suprapatellar pouch on a supine lateral radiograph: an articular fracture must be present. Haemarthrosis without fracture often accompanies injury to the anterior cruciate ligament.

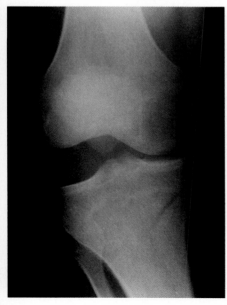

Fig. 97 Ligament rupture is often less painful than a ligament strain. A tense effusion does not occur because the fluid escapes through the torn capsule into the surrounding tissues. Ligament laxity can be demonstrated on examination and recorded by a stress X-ray. An incomplete tear (strain) is painful on stressing but there is no laxity.

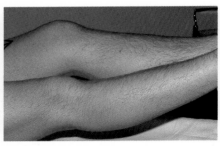

Fig. 98 Meniscus tear. A twisting injury on the flexed knee may catch a meniscus between the joint surfaces and tear it. A bucket-handle tear (left) usually presents with a locked knee, in which the torn fragment prevents full extension of the joint (right). Alternatively, there may be recurrent pain, swelling and locking. Both these presentations are best managed by arthroscopy and (if possible) arthroscopic meniscectomy.

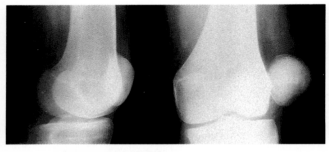

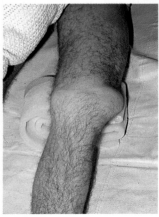

Fig. 99 Patellar dislocation. A tear in the medial patellar retinacula allows the patella to jump laterally over the femoral condyle.

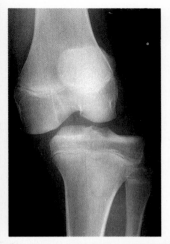

Fig. 100 Dislocation of the knee is rare: the popliteal artery may be injured.

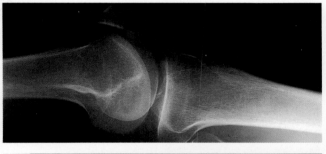

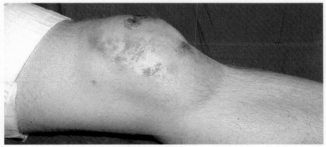

Fig. 101 Patellar fracture results from a direct blow or occurs as part of a disruption of the extensor mechanism. The gap may be palpable but is obscured later by swelling. Restoration of the articular surface and continuity of the extensor mechanism is the aim of treatment.

Leg

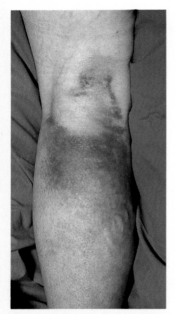

Fig. 102 Rupture of a popliteal cyst into the calf may cause extensive bruising (upper) or mimic deep venous thrombosis. The arthrogram (lower) shows contrast passing from the cyst into the calf.

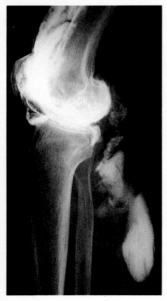

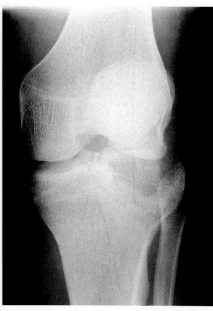

Fig. 103 Fracture of the tibial plateau occurs when an abduction or adduction force drives the femoral condyle into the tibia. The articular surface is depressed and fragmented. The extent of the injury is often under-estimated on standard X-rays (upper) and is best seen on tomography. If possible, the articular surface should be elevated, supported with bone graft and stabilized by internal fixation (lower).

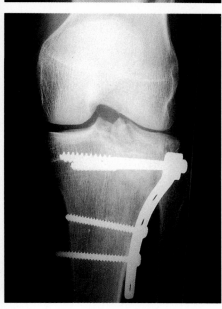

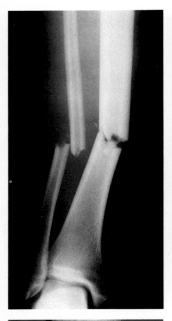

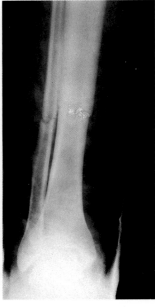

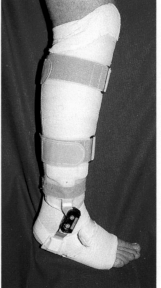

Fig. 104 Fractures of the tibial shaft are common. Because of its subcutaneous position the fracture is often open and there may be considerable damage to the skin and soft tissues. Tibial shaft fractures which are stable (mild displacement and transverse fracture line) can be treated in a long cast (upper left and right) replaced by a below-knee cast or removeable brace after three to four weeks (lower).

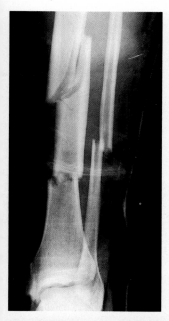

Fig. 105 Unstable fractures often lose alignment and length in a cast (left) and need close observation. Internal fixation may be necessary (lower).

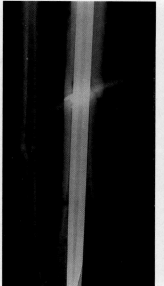

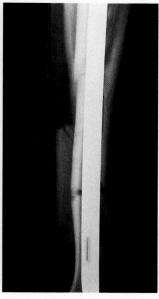

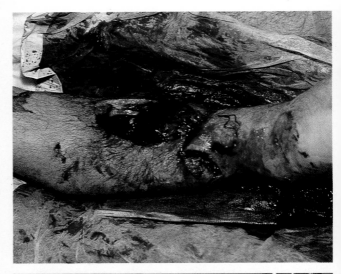

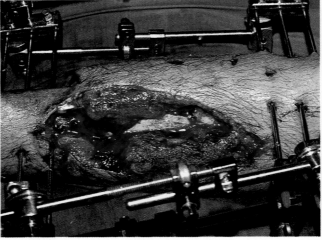

Fig. 106 Unstable open fractures are often stabilized by an external fixation device, which allows access to the wound and avoids placing implants in a contaminated wound.

Ankle and Foot

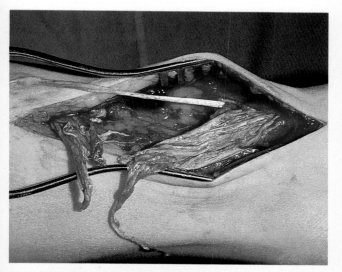

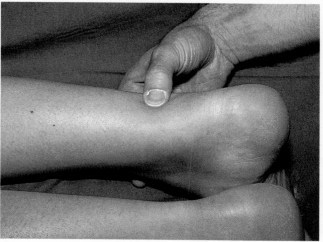

Fig. 107 Middle-aged athletes may suffer Achilles tendon rupture (upper). The patient often believes he has been struck from behind, for example by a squash racquet. A gap is palpable 3-5cm above the insertion but may be obscured by swelling (lower). Weak active plantar flexion can be produced by the other posterior muscles but the patient cannot stand on tiptoe. Squeezing the calf causes plantar flexion of the ankle if the Achilles tendon is intact but not if it is ruptured (Simmonds' test).

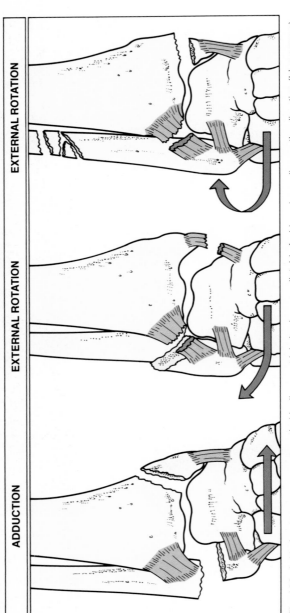

ADDUCTION   **EXTERNAL ROTATION**   **EXTERNAL ROTATION**

Fig. 108 Ankle fractures are accompanied by ligament injuries in a predictable fashion, depending on the direction (blue arrows) and violence of the injury. If the fibula is broken above the joint line, or if there is swelling and tenderness over both sides of the joint,¹ the possibility of instability with lateral shift of the talus should be born in mind.

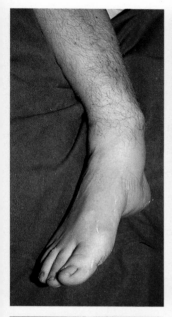

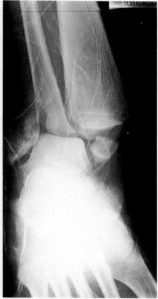

Fig. 109 Displaced ankle fractures should be reduced accurately: this often requires open reduction and internal fixation.

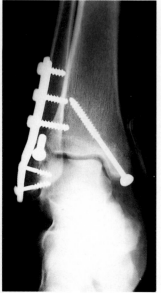

69

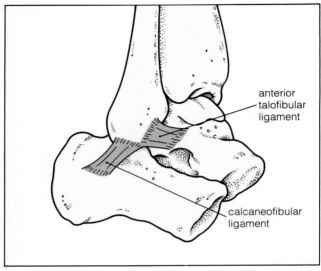

anterior
talofibular
ligament

calcaneofibular
ligament

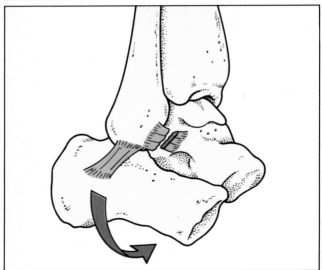

Fig. 110 An ankle sprain is a tear of the anterolateral ligament, usually caused by an inversion injury. Forced adduction of the plantar-flexed ankle tears the anterior talofibular ligament, and occasionally the calcaneofibular ligament also. There is swelling and tenderness anterior to and below the lateral malleolus.

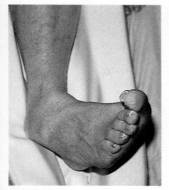

Fig. 111 Fractures and fracture-dislocations of the talus, as seen here, are caused by violent dorsiflexion. Displaced fractures should be reduced accurately and stabilised by internal fixation. Avascular necrosis of the body of the talus may occur.

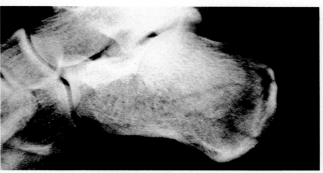

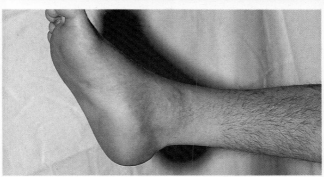

Fig. 112 Calcaneal fractures are disabling and usually result from a fall from a height. The bone is crushed and the fracture often extends into its subtalar articular surface. The degree of pain and swelling usually requires admission to hospital for elevation. Characteristic bruising appears in the sole after a few days.

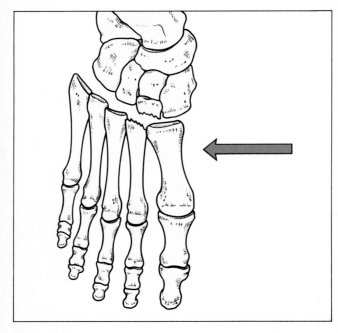

Fig. 113 Like carpal dislocations, tarsal and tarsometatarsal dislocations are easy to miss. A severely swollen foot after injury should arouse suspicion and prompt a request for oblique radiographs together with a view of the opposite foot for comparison. Tarsometatarsal fracture-dislocations may be complicated by vascular injury.

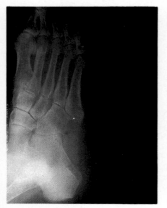

Fig. 114 The most common foot fracture affects the base of the 5th metatarsal, where the peroneus brevis tendon inserts and avulses a piece of bone when the foot is forcibly inverted. The site of tenderness will distinguish this injury from an ankle sprain. Like most metatarsal and phalangeal fractures, treatment is directed at pain relief and early return of function. If necessary, a walking cast for two weeks improves comfort.

INDEX